C000311626

THE ROSARY PRIEST

THE
ROSARY PRIEST

A Biography of
Patrick Peyton CSC

Fr Tom Mulligan

VERITAS

First published 2018 by
Veritas Publications
7–8 Lower Abbey Street, Dublin 1, Ireland
publications@veritas.ie
www.veritas.ie

ISBN 978 1 84730 861 0

Copyright © Tom Mulligan, 2018

10 9 8 7 6 5 4 3 2 1

The material in this publication is protected by copyright law.
Except as may be permitted by law, no part of the material may be
reproduced (including by storage in a retrieval system) or
transmitted in any form or by any means, adapted, rented or lent
without the written permission of the copyright owners.
Applications for permissions should be addressed to the publisher.

*A catalogue record for this book
is available from the British Library.*

Veritas would like to thank Holy Cross Family Ministries for
permission to include a selection of photographs from their archive.

Designed by Colette Dower, Veritas Publications
Printed in the Republic of Ireland by Walsh Colour Print, Kerry

*Veritas books are printed on paper made from the wood pulp of
managed forests. For every tree felled, at least one tree is planted,
thereby renewing natural resources.*

In memory of my parents,
Margaret and Tom Mulligan,
who signed the 'Rosary Pledge',
and my brother John Francis

Acknowledgements

I wish to thank all at the Father Patrick Peyton Memorial Centre, Attymass, for their co-operation.

I am grateful also to Daragh Reddin and Donna Doherty at Veritas for their encouragement and support.

CONTENTS

FOREWORD

On 18 December 2017, Pope Francis solemnly declared Servant of God Fr Patrick Joseph Peyton CSC to be venerable. This designation represented a rare recognition by the universal Church that Fr Peyton was a person of heroic virtue whose life was worthy of veneration. The announcement was warmly welcomed in Ireland, but most especially by the people of Attymass in Co. Mayo, where he was born and raised. The news of his elevation, however, came as no great surprise to them, for they have long regarded him as a saint.

From 1942 to 1992, Fr Peyton travelled the globe championing the importance of family prayer with his mantra, 'the family that prays together stays together'. An Irish immigrant to the United States, he experienced a miraculous recovery from tuberculosis through, what he believed to be, the intercession of the Blessed Virgin Mary. In gratitude for his recovery, Fr Peyton initiated an international programme to promote family prayer and specifically the Rosary.

Father Peyton was one of the first to pioneer the use of mass media to evangelise; he utilised film, radio, outdoor advertising and television, with the help of a who's who of Hollywood celebrities, to spread his message. Most famously, he conducted a series of international Rosary crusades, in more than forty countries, addressing in person more than twenty-six million people worldwide.

He was a man of extraordinary faith, who, through his simple message sincerely conveyed, never failed to touch the hearts of his listeners. As a dedicated man, and a Spirit-filled priest, who exercised his ministry faithfully and with enormous commitment, Patrick Peyton is an inspiring example to people of faith everywhere.

INTRODUCTION

The Scottish theologian John Macquarrie describes the devout Celt as a 'very much God-intoxicated person whose life was embraced on all sides by the divine Being'.[1] Father Patrick Peyton was very much a God-intoxicated man, who offered himself completely 'as a holy sacrifice, truly pleasing to God' (Rm 12:1). Like Mary, he was fully dedicated to the fulfilment of the destiny to which God had called him. His approach to God was invariably through Mary, who leads us to her son.

Father Peyton was a tireless evangelist, a man of tremendous zeal, who traversed the globe to give witness to Christ, who had bequeathed his mother to us from the cross (cf. Jn 19:27). In what he termed 'his testimony' he declared:

> I … give witness to the power of God who, through his Blessed Mother, restored my strength … [and] who placed me on a road where I could continually give testimony to his mercy and to the sensitive love his Mother has for all of us.[2]

At a time when many preachers sought to instil fear in their congregations, Fr Peyton's message was always one of love: the love of God, the love of Mary our mother for her children, who wished to lead them to her son. Everyone appreciated his simplicity and his humility, but it was his utter sincerity that most attracted people. All realised that Peyton believed what he proclaimed with every fibre of his being.

His special qualities were well observed by one journalist:

> Those acquainted with Fr Peyton will, perhaps, agree that if there is one secret of his success it is … that love glows and sometimes blazes on his broad, innocent face. It exalts his plain speech … It is equipment enough. Even those with no piety toward Mary appear to recognise and revere the love that this man brings.[3]

This study will include references to aspects of the Irish faith tradition, which still influence us today. We are, as Michael Maher reminds us, the product of everything that has been done and endured in our country across the centuries: 'In spite of the cultural gap that lies between us and our ancestors we are united with them, and many of the attitudes and feelings that motivated them are unconsciously in our bones, even if not consciously in our minds.'[4] The great saints of Ireland, and the men and women of learning and vision who helped form our religious outlook, 'are a part of the living stream to which we belong'.[5]

In the global Church, Fr Peyton was a priest of significant influence. Throughout his long ministry he enjoyed the support and encouragement of four pontiffs, Pius XII, John XXIII, Paul VI and John Paul II, all of whom corresponded with him. As a priest who travelled extensively, he became well acquainted with many of the great Church figures of his day, including Cardinal Suenens (Belgium), Dom Hélder Câmara (Brazil), Saint Óscar Romero (San Salvador) and Mother Teresa of Calcutta (Kolkata).

At the Second Vatican Council he successfully lobbied the bishops to have statements on family prayer included in two influential documents, the 'Pastoral Constitution of the Church in the Modern World' or *Gaudium et Spes*, and the 'Decree on the Apostolate of the Laity', *Apostolicam Actuositatem*. Furthermore, it was a letter from Fr Peyton which prompted Pope Paul VI to issue *Marialis Cultus*, an Apostolic Exhortation – 'For the Right Ordering and Development of Devotion to the Blessed Virgin Mary' – in 1974. He was also actively involved as a lobbyist and advisor at the 1980 Synod of Bishops on the Family in Rome; several prelates, including Archbishop John Quinn of San Francisco, consulted him about the Family Rosary Crusade. Because of Fr Peyton's efforts, the Synod endorsed the Rosary as a form of family prayer in its final document.

CHAPTER 1

THE EARLY YEARS

Patrick Joseph Peyton, the sixth of nine children (four boys and five girls) of John Peyton and Mary Gillard, was born on 9 January 1909, in the townland of Carracastle, near Ballina in Co. Mayo. On the following day he was baptised in St Joseph's parish church, Attymass, by Fr Walter Henry PP. His father, John Peyton, the eldest of sixteen children of James Peyton and Bridget Ginley, was born in 1868 in the same house. John had married Mary Gillard of Rathreedane, from the neighbouring parish of Bonniconlon, in March 1899. Mary was the granddaughter of Robert Gillard, a French soldier who had stayed on in Ireland in 1798, after Napoleon's forces – led by General Humbert – made an unsuccessful attempt to free the country from British rule.

Patrick was born when Ireland was still feeling the effects of the Great Famine (1845–51). This catastrophe, which resulted in part, from the protracted failure of the potato crop, would still have been a living memory for some in Attymass during Pat's childhood. In what was arguably the single greatest disaster in Irish history, 1.1 million people lost their lives and a further one million emigrated.

The potato blight was a virulent, airborne disease, first detected in the eastern United States, in 1843. Its arrival in Ireland was confirmed by the Botanic Gardens, Glasnevin, Dublin, on 20 August 1845. By the beginning of September of that year it had spread countrywide.[1]

Attymass was, as it happens, the first parish in the country to officially report deaths directly due to the Famine; on 19 November 1846, Fr Michael O' Flynn PP, Attymass wrote to the local Justice of the Peace informing him of the deaths from hunger of four persons.[2]

In a letter to the Lord Lieutenant of Ireland, dated 30 October 1847, Fr Bernard Egan, the parish priest of Bonniconlon, which neighbours Attymass, described both parishes as among the most destitute in the county:

> These two parishes are situated at the foot of the Ox Mountains and consist principally of reclaimable bog and mountain with a small proportion of arable land. The two successive failures of the potato crop have reduced a large number of the inhabitants to an awful state of destitution … The small crop of potatoes planted in the present year in this district … have unfortunately been attacked with the disease which destroyed former crops and are not now available for food. It has been and is now admitted by several government officers and others employed under the Board of Works that this district is, with scarcely an exception, the most impoverished and destitute in the entire county of Mayo.[3]

'*An Gorta Mór*' – The Great Hunger – wreaked havoc in Attymass; census data reveals that the population of Attymass parish, which was three thousand four hundred and thirty-five in 1841, was reduced to two thousand four hundred and thirty-one by 1851.[4] Many hundreds of people died while many others took to the emigrant ships. In an interview with *The Nation* newspaper, Fr Michael Flynn PP revealed that in one six-month period alone, from 1 October 1846 to 1 April 1847, three hundred and twenty parishioners had perished, of whom two hundred and forty had died of hunger.[5]

It was not until 1885 that a fungicide was discovered in France called the 'Bordeaux mixture', made up of copper sulphate (bluestone), slaked lime and water which, when applied to healthy plants, afforded protection from the blight. Pat remembered, as a young boy, seeing his mother tending the crops when his father was ill:

> I recall seeing her out in the field spraying the potatoes, a job that had to be done twice or maybe three times in June and July, depending on the weather and the incidence of the blight. The metal knapsack sprayer with its hand operated pump held nearly four gallons of spray. As a child I would help to mix the lime and copper sulphate in the barrel of water at the end of the potato field and ladle the mixture into the sprayer. She would then hoist it on her back and march up and down the rows of potatoes to cover the stalks with the blue liquid, a task which on each occasion required several gruelling days of effort to complete.[6]

Pat was raised in a loving family in a three-room thatched cottage on a twelve-acre farm, from which the family eked out a living. Thanks mainly to the efforts of the Land League, founded in 1879 and led by Michael Davitt and Charles Stewart Parnell, whose watchword was 'the Land for the People', the old landlordism had been largely abolished by the turn of the century, and Ireland had become a country of owner-occupiers. This radical change in the ownership of the land has been characterised by historians as the greatest revolution in modern Ireland.[7]

The Peyton family engaged in typical mixed farming. They kept a horse for the farm work, raised cattle, pigs, chickens, turkeys, ducks and geese, grew potatoes, oats, turnips, cabbage and onions. Pat's father, John Peyton, as a boy, drove long hours through the night with his horse and cart, taking milk to Swinford to sell, with his mother beside him to keep him company. Later, John worked as a stonemason, building homes and stables in the locality. In addition, he also found employment with the county council maintaining local roads. Like many Irish men of his time, John Peyton often spent summers and autumns in England, doing farm work. Meanwhile, at home, Mary and her children tended the farm, saved the crops and harvested turf from the bog for fuel.

The most important crop was the potato. Despite the Famine, it had continued to be the staple food which guaranteed the people a crop that would keep their stomachs full nearly all year round. The land was ploughed or turned with a loy or spade soon after St Patrick's Day, when the soil had dried out enough to be worked. Holes were opened at regular intervals in the ridges using a dibbling stick or '*stíbhín*'. A slit potato, with an 'eye' or bud, dusted with lime, was dropped into every hole and covered with soil. Later came two mouldings with layers of earth, the first spread before the stalks emerged, the next carefully deposited around the young stalks. In due course the stalks were sprayed as necessary. The first potatoes were traditionally dug on Garland Sunday, the last Sunday in July. In October and early November, the main crop had to be dug, picked and stored in pits to provide sufficient nourishment for the household, and for pigs and poultry until the following June.

Father Peyton remembered his mother as a woman who radiated peace, joy and love of family. In his childhood she was the very centre of his world; he had no other horizon, no other focus but her face, and no other sense of security except her arms that took him when he needed her. His mother was full of fun also, always ready for a prank or a joke. The children were never afraid of her. They could confide their secrets to her and count on her to win them little privileges, that they would hesitate to ask directly of their father.

The work was hard, but there were some compensations. In his autobiography, Fr Peyton fondly recalled a fine day in the bog:

> There was no day in all one's life to match that special day on the bog when nature regretted the long series of buffeting to which it normally subjected us in Mayo, and the sun smiled, and the breeze laughed, and humming bees danced in the fragrant heather and a skylark praised God infinitely high in the limpid air. On such a day the

mid-afternoon meal became a banquet such as no cordon-bleu chef has ever served. We would gather dry sods of turf to start a fire, draw water from a well or stream, prepare the tea in a tin can, and serve it in mugs.[8]

John Peyton was a devoted husband and father, who did his best to make ends meet for the family, but at the age of forty-two he was struck down with a chronic form of asthma, so debilitating that by the time the last child was born in 1916, he was unable to do a full day's work. He was forced to restrict himself to supervision and direction, riding the horse out to the fields to watch while the rest of the family worked. Eventually, the need for more income forced the three eldest girls, Beatrice, Mary, and Ellen (known as Nellie), to emigrate to the United States, settling in Scranton, Pennsylvania, near where other members of the Gillard family had settled a few years earlier. At home, all the remaining family pitched in, taking up the slack caused by the absence of John and his three eldest children.

In his preaching, many years later, Fr Peyton described how, as a child, he was in awe of his father; a tall, powerfully-built man, with a heavy moustache and deep penetrating eyes. Seeing this 'extraordinary man'[9] get on his knees to lead the Rosary every evening and hearing him announce nightly, 'I believe in God ...' made a deep and lasting impression on the young boy. The nightly recitation of the Rosary was a formative experience for Pat, one that stayed with him all his life:

If there was one inflexible rule in our home, it was that every one of us had to participate in the family Rosary led by my father. It didn't matter how hard or how long the day's work – digging potatoes, cutting turf or repairing a road. Often one or another would drop to sleep on his knees. But he was always brought back into prayer, kindly but firmly. It was the entire family praising God, asking him through his mother to protect it, to guide it to the destiny he had intended for it. That nightly scene constitutes my earliest memory and the most abiding. From it I derive the entire pattern and purpose of my existence.[10]

The nightly Rosary provided the spiritual nourishment that was as necessary as their daily food. The fruits of family prayer were visible in the spirit of unity and charity that existed among them.

As I look back over the nineteen years spent in that poor little home, I cannot recall an unpleasant moment. There were times when we had little or nothing to eat, but there were never times when we did not have our strong spirit of faith to face all the difficulties and hardships of life. Not only did my parents ... teach us the great truths and virtues of our faith by their words, but they lived these truths and virtues before our very eyes. A great spirit of charity and unity dwelt in that home; brothers and sisters never lost an opportunity to come to the aid of their parents or each other.[11]

John Peyton took his role as head of the household very seriously. He was strict with his children but never resorted to corporal punishment, which was used in many homes and in all schools at the time. In addition to the Rosary, John prayed a specific prayer every day for the welfare and protection of the family.

> O most loving Jesus ...
>
> Remember that this family belongs to you, for to you we have in a specific way dedicated and devoted ourselves.
>
> Look upon us in your loving kindness. Preserve us from every danger. Give us help in time of need.
>
> And grant us your grace to persevere to the end in imitation of the Holy Family, that having revered you and loved you faithfully on earth, we may bless and praise you eternally in heaven.
>
> O Mary, most sweet mother, to your intercession we have recourse, knowing your divine Son will hear your prayers ...
>
> Jesus, Mary and Joseph, enlighten us, help us, and save us.[12]

Pat learned much from his father, including a sense of integrity and a strong work ethic, but most important of all was the living faith that John Peyton had imbued in his children, which he expressed daily through family prayer. Prayer was as natural to him as breathing the air:

> I did not appreciate what it was for the heart of a man to be in love with God, but my father showed us – not by telling it to us, but by doing it – for we were used to seeing that man on his knees in the morning, and again at four o'clock in the afternoon, and again at night when he led the Rosary. He had such living faith that he expected everybody to have the same.[13]

It was his concern for their moral welfare that made John Peyton dead set against any of the family going to England. During his own various trips there, he had seen how some young Irish people had abandoned their moral principles and religious practice once they were away from the supports and safeguards of home.

Pat was so accustomed to the nightly family Rosary at home that he missed it greatly when he stayed for a time with a family in an adjoining townland. It happened that a farmer needed a youngster to help pick potatoes for a week and Pat was glad to oblige. He arrived in good time on a Monday morning for work, for which he would be paid two shillings a day. The farmer hitched his horse to a plough and ploughed out the potato drills.

His wife and Pat followed with buckets, gathering the potatoes and dumping them into pits, where they were covered with straw and clay to protect from frost. After supper, as they sat around the turf fire, Pat gradually realised that this home was not like his own. He sat on later than his usual bedtime, heavy with sleep after the day's work, but hoping to hear the man of the house say: 'It's getting late, isn't it? Let's get on our knees and say the Rosary to thank God and his Blessed Mother for watching over us this day.' But the words never came. Young Pat was very taken aback.

While he pretended to sleep, he said his own Rosary and felt the pangs of homesickness. For the rest of the week he was more withdrawn than usual and, as he worked alongside the farmer and his family, he found it difficult to join freely in their conversations. He found it hard to come to terms with the fact that they talked together, laughed together, lived together, but did not pray together. Afterwards, he reproached himself for judging them:

> Gradually an idea formed itself in my simple mind. I had no right to condemn these people. It was no wickedness on their part, nothing more than a lack of knowledge. Nobody had ever explained to them what a difference it made to kneel together in front of the hearth and tie the family together with God and Our Lady and the saints. I could see my duty clearly. It was not to be bitter or to be morose. It was to explain to this man what he was missing, what he was failing to give his children.[14]

Pat, who in adulthood became known as the Rosary Priest and the American Apostle of the Rosary, finally got the courage to speak as the farmer paid him his week's wages. The farmer heard him out and later Pat learned that his family started saying the Rosary and kept on saying it.

John Peyton, who spoke Irish and English fluently, would, from childhood, have been immersed in Irish spirituality. God's presence was felt in the daily round of human tasks. His help was always close by: *'Is gaire cabhair Dé ná an doras'* ('God's help is nearer than the door'). The people considered no moment of life, no action of the day, to be without bearing on their relationship with God. The language of the people was sprinkled with expressions of piety. Such expressions as 'God save all here', 'God bless the work', *'Le cúnamh Dé'* ('With the help of God') were very common.

In addition, there were prayers for all occasions, from getting up, to kindling the fire, to going to work, to passing a cemetery. These traditional prayers were very numerous. One collection of five hundred and thirty-nine such folk-prayers was published in 1974 by Fr Diarmuid Ó Laoghaire SJ. The following is a night prayer which was collected in Killasser parish, which neighbours Attymass:

> *Go mbeirimid beo ar an am seo arís,*
> *Fé shaoghal agus fé shláinte*
> *I ngrádh Dé agus in ngrádh na gcomharsan*
> *Dé lus an peacadh is lugha agus an grásta is mó.*
>
> May we still be alive at this time again,
> Full of life and health
> In God's love and in the neighbour's love
> Fruit of the smallest sin and the greatest grace.[15]

Devotion to Mary featured very prominently in the Irish tradition over many centuries. The full-page image of the Virgin on folio 7v of the Book of Kells, dating from the eighth century, is the earliest surviving image of the Virgin Mary in a Western manuscript. The image depicts a tender moment between mother and child, with the Virgin enthroned and the infant Christ on her lap. Mary's mantle is purple, the colour of royalty. The dominant position of the Virgin demonstrates the high respect with which she was treated. The halo around her head bears three crosses that link her to the Trinity and suggests not only Mary's sanctity but also her role in salvation. Mary's halo celebrates her as the Mother of God, while the absence of a halo around Christ's head emphasises his humanity.[16]

The first written reference to Mary is in a Gaelic prophecy dated c.617 in which Brigid is called 'another Mary'. Devotion to the Mother of God found mature expression in hymns and prayers dating back to the eighth century. Cú Chuimne, a monk of Iona (c.747), composed 'Cantemus in omni die', ('Let us sing everyday') a hymn of thirteen verses, said to be the finest Hiberno-Latin hymn in honour of Our Lady:

> In alternate measures chanting daily we sing Mary's praise
>
> And in strains of glad rejoicing, to the Lord our voices raise.
>
> By a woman's disobedience, eating the forbidden tree,

Was the world betrayed and ruined, was by
woman's aid set free.

Clad in helmet of salvation, clad in breastplate
shining bright.

May the hand of Mary guide us to the realms of
endless light.[17]

Again Blathmac, a mid-eighth century poet from the east
Monaghan area, composed several long poems in the Irish
language to Our Lady, one of which begins:

Come to me, loving Mary,
that I may keen with you your very dear one
Alas! That your Son should go to the cross,
he who was a great diadem, a beautiful hero.[18]

The earliest litany of Mary in the Irish language is found
in *An Leabhar Breac* (The Speckled Book), a fifteenth-
century manuscript from east Galway. The litany,
however, cannot be later than the twelfth century.

O great Mary,
O greatest of Mary's,
O paragon of women,
O queen of the angels,
O lady of heaven,
O lady full and overflowing with the grace of the
Holy Spirit,
O blessed and more than blessed one,

O mother of eternal glory,
O mother of the Church in heaven and earth,
O mother of affection and forgiveness,
O mother of the golden light,
O honour of the ether,
O sign of gentleness,
O gate of heaven,
O golden casket,
O bed of kindness and compassion,
O temple of the deity,
O beauty of virgins,
O lady of the nations,
O fountain of the gardens
O cleansing of sins,
O washing of souls
O mother of orphans,
O breast of infants,
O consolation of the wretched,
O star of the sea,
O handmaid of God,
O mother of Christ,
O spouse of the Lord,
O beauteous as a dove,
O lovely as the moon,
O elect as the sun,
O repulse of Eve's reproach,
O renewal of life,
O beauty of women,
O chief of virgins,
O garden enclosed,
O sealed fountain,

O mother of God,
O perpetual virgin,
O holy virgin,
O prudent virgin,
O beauteous virgin,
O chaste virgin,
O temple of the living God,
O throne of the eternal King,
O sanctuary of the Holy Ghost,
O virgin of the stem of Jesse,
O crimson rose of the land of Jacob,
O cedar of Lebanon,
O cypress of Zion,
O flourishing as a palm
O fruitful as an olive tree,
O glorious Son-bearer,
O light of Nazareth,
O beauty of the world,
O highborn of Christian people,
O queen of the world,
O ladder of heaven.[19]

The name 'Muire' is and has been, since the thirteenth century, especially reserved for the Mother of God. We are the inheritors of a great and healthy tradition about Our Lady and, in that tradition, she was never separated from her son. Even in our everyday greetings in Irish we link both names – *Dia is Muire duit* – and for example, in the following verse and proverb:

A Mhuire na ngrás, a Mháthair Mhic Dé, Go gcuire tú ar mo leas mé. (Mother of graces, Mother of God's Son, May you set me on the right course.)[20]

Tá Dia láidir is máthair maith aige. (God is strong and has a good mother.)

The Rosary held an exceptionally high place in Irish religious practice since the penal days. It was usually offered in union with the Mass. A common introduction was:

> We offer up this Rosary to the honour and in the name of Jesus and to the honour of the glorious Virgin Mary, to share in the Holy Sacrifice of the Mass, with the same intention with which our Saviour offered himself on the tree of the Cross for us; for the intention of the Pope and the Catholic Church; for every poor soul that is suffering most severely the pains of purgatory, and especially our own dead.[21]

It was, of course, also offered as a family prayer in the home, as it was in the Peyton household.

Pat's primary education began in May 1914 when, at the age of five, he enrolled in Bofield National School. Four years later, while he was living with his maternal grandparents in Bonniconlon, he attended the local school near their home. Later, on his return to Carracastle he resumed his education in Bofield. He left this school at the age of fourteen because of an incident with the principal,

Tadhg O'Leary, and was enrolled in Currower National School, not far from his home. In 1924 Pat left school and returned to work on the family farm. He was fifteen years old.

It was common practice at the time in Ireland for one or another of the children in a family to live for a period in the home of a relative. So it was for the young Pat, who, on two occasions, enjoyed extended stays with his maternal grandparents, Robert and Kitty Gillard in Bonniconlon. Pat was deeply influenced by both, but more especially by his grandfather Robert, who had been blind for twenty years. Despite his infirmity he demonstrated the power of faith by his intense love of prayer, particularly the Rosary, and his serene acceptance of his physical condition. When others went to Sunday Mass, Robert, though advanced in years, dressed in his best clothes, knelt at a chair and prayed fifteen decades of the Rosary.

Pat had fond memories of his time with his grandparents in Bonniconlon. Because of his blindness, his grandfather could not be left on his own, so it often fell to Pat to keep an eye on him, while the others were out at work. Pat was glad to oblige for he enjoyed the company of old people and being of assistance to his grandfather.

> In retrospect, the period I then spent with him was very important in my life. Dominick Melvin, the village blacksmith, was a frequent visitor. Nell Gallagher, a neighbour, would come in at night to sit by the hearth and smoke her short clay pipe

when her work was finished, and her husband Patrick would sometimes come with her. Then my grandmother would light up my grandfather's clay pipe for him, and the conversation would range far and wide, always eloquent. As I sat spellbound in the warm recess of the fireplace, I learned things about the family and the community which otherwise I'd probably never have known.[22]

Back home in Carracastle each Sunday, Holy Day and First Friday, the Peyton family walked the four miles to Attymass Church to attend Mass, despite the frequently inclement weather. Pat regularly served two Masses each Sunday, the one attended by his family and a second Mass two hours later. He delighted in fulfilling his duties as a Mass server, lighting candles, swinging the incense burner and answering the Latin responses.

Parish missions, which were held every three years, made a deep impression on Pat and helped to awaken in him a vocation to the priesthood. A 'lonely impulse of delight'[23] filled his mind and heart. He would devote his whole life to the service of God as a missionary priest. Later in life he recalled how he longed to be a priest by any means. He was willing to go to Africa to work on the foreign missions. He realised, of course, that his own family did not have the resources to finance his seminary training.

He wrote first to the Capuchins but received no acknowledgement. His parish priest, Fr Roger O'Donnell, wrote on his behalf to the Society of African Missions, asking that Pat be admitted as a scholarship student, but he was informed that he did not have sufficient education to start the seminary programme. He was so deeply disappointed that he abandoned all thoughts of priesthood.

CHAPTER 2

EXILES IN AMERICA

In the years immediately following this setback – his teenage years – Pat became frustrated, stubborn and quick tempered. His chances of steady employment at home were very poor indeed and he had little or no opportunity of furthering his education. The only role he could now see for himself in Ireland was that of a stone breaker; his future lay in laboriously breaking rocks into pebble-sized fragments with his hammer to fill the holes in the road. One day when he had been out working with a horse and cart repairing a road, he quarreled with his father. In a temper he abandoned the horse and cart, and took off across the fields.

In *All for Her* he confessed:

> I had no idea where I was going, but I figured I'd spend the night in a neighbour's house and strike out for somewhere, Ballina or Dublin or England, the next day. I didn't go very far, however; my sister had been watching from the door, knowing my mood, and she came after me up the hill until she finally persuaded me to stop my foolishness and come back home. I know my father must have been very upset, but he gave absolutely no indication, nor did he ever again refer to the matter.[1]

With such poor prospects in Ireland, his thoughts turned to emigration. His older brother Tom was thinking along the same lines. They both knew well that their father would not permit them to go to England. They hoped, however, that he would be more open to them emigrating to the USA as his own three brothers had done before them and since their three older sisters – Beatrice, Mary and Ellen (Nellie) – had at this stage settled there also.

An opportunity to raise the matter with his father occurred one sunny afternoon in June 1927, when Pat and his brother Tom were in the fields thinning turnips. Their father, taking advantage of the fine day, strolled down the road in the sunshine to admire the soft green leaves of the turnip plants and chat with his sons as they worked. Pat talked quickly and succeeded in overcoming his father's reluctance to let them leave home. Finally, it was agreed that they would write to their sisters in Scranton, to see if they might send the passage money and sponsor their visas.

The brothers had to present themselves at the American consulate in Dublin to obtain their visas. The trip to the capital city was itself a great adventure, as neither of them had ever travelled far from home. In his nineteen years Pat had travelled no further than Ballina and Bonniconlon, except twice, once when he went by bus to Bundoran, Co. Donegal, about fifty miles north, and again when he helped a neighbour bring cattle to the fair in Foxford, seven or eight miles away in the foothills of the Ox Mountains. He had never been on a train before, so it was with an air of great anticipation that he boarded what he called 'the iron monster' at Ballina.

As he headed east, he marvelled at the quality of the land, when he left behind the rocky hillsides and the bogs of Connacht. The towns along the way, Claremorris, Athlone, Mullingar, each seemed like hubs of excitement and promise, an anticipation of what lay ahead of him. When they reached Dublin, snow was falling, and they were dazzled by the bright lights of the great city. They were impressed by the double-decker buses, the endless lines of shops and the throngs of people walking the streets. Pat was convinced that he was going to have a great life once he reached America. Then he would be up with the best of them, with their fine clothes and their fine homes. Having completed their business at the embassy they returned to Carracastle to finalise arrangements for their leave-taking.

As the day of their departure drew near Pat noticed that his father was somewhat troubled. On the Sunday before they set out, Pat was alone in the house with his parents, when his father called him into the bedroom. 'Go down on your knees,' he said, 'and make a promise here before the picture of the Sacred Heart. From now on there will be nobody but yourself to advise you and to decide for you. But your first responsibility will always be to save your soul, and so I want you to promise to be faithful to Our Lord in America.'[2]

On the morning of their departure, 13 May 1928, they had to leave home in good time to catch the early train from Ballina, which would take them all the way through Tuam, Limerick, Cork and on to Cobh, where they would board the liner for America. Michael, the eldest, and his mother set out for the station in the horse and cart, carrying the few pieces of luggage containing their personal belongings. Pat and Tom followed on two bicycles. At the turn of the road, Pat paused to look back and caught a last glimpse of his father standing motionless, alone at the half door of their cottage; he was not well enough to accompany them to the station. At that moment he recalled his father's advice, 'Be faithful to Our Lord in America'.

In later years Fr Peyton remarked, 'My father, that blessed man, did not say to me "Go to America and become wealthy." No, he gave the best advice a father could ever give a son. It was the last advice my blessed father ever gave to me, for he died six years later, and I never saw him again.'[3]

They bade farewell to their mother at the station. Michael supported her as she continued to wave her handkerchief as the train pulled out, while her sons waved back from the train, for as long as they could catch a glimpse of her. Years later, Fr Peyton remembered how that morning his heart was crushed with sorrow, and tears blinded his eyes. As the train sped towards Foxford he was still thinking of his mother, huddled in the cart driving back to Carracastle, her black shawl drawn tightly around her shoulders, to hide her misery.

The voyage to America took ten days. Having made a quick stop in Boston their ship arrived in New York on 23 May. The brothers immediately took a ferry to Hoboken, New Jersey, and from there travelled by train to Scranton where they were greeted by their sisters and brother-in-law, Michael Gallagher husband of Beatrice, from Crossmolina, Co. Mayo. The brothers made their home with the Gallaghers, who welcomed them with open arms.

Still smarting from his rejections in Ireland, Pat had at this point banished from his mind all thoughts of a religious vocation. His ambition now was to become a wealthy man, as a dealer in property. But first he had to find employment to meet his living expenses and to repay his sisters on whom he depended so much. Like most Irish emigrants of their generation, however, they were unskilled, with little formal education.

Tom quickly found employment in the coalmines alongside Michael Gallagher, but Pat had to wait six long weeks to find suitable work. In the end, it was through the good offices of his sister Nellie that he found a job as caretaker in St Peter's Cathedral, Scranton. Nellie was acquainted with the rector, Monsignor Paul Kelly, and secretly arranged for Pat to meet with him regarding the vacancy. Nellie always had the welfare of her brother Pat at heart and firmly believed that he was called to be a priest. Pat was to take up his new job in the cathedral on 1 July.

In the meantime, he got temporary work on a building site. Later, when Pat heard that two men were to be laid off, one of whom had a family to support, he volunteered to leave in his place, saying he had another job lined up.

'You're a fool,' the boss told him. 'You can stay here and make good money.'

Pat shook his head. 'No,' he replied, 'it would not be right for me to take a job away from a family man.'[4]

Later, he learned that the construction boss had juggled the work to keep both men employed, so impressed was he by Pat's concern for them. Pat was very glad that his post in the cathedral made him economically independent and enabled him to contribute his share to the upkeep of the Gallagher household, with whom Tom and he were staying.

Working in the cathedral had an extraordinary effect on Pat. He never felt alone, even when the church was empty. The joy and peace and the sense of being at home, which he used to experience in Attymass church, all flooded back into his soul. As he swept, dusted or polished, he would turn towards the tabernacle on the altar and greet our Lord, hidden sacramentally behind the veil. When he passed the statue of the Blessed Mother, he stopped and talked to her. Later he explained, 'Being alone in … that big church in that holy house of God – before Jesus Christ and the blessed Sacrament – the longing to be a priest once more overwhelmed me.'[5]

Experiencing the call of God so strongly, one day he decided to make another effort to pursue his vocation:

> I was behind the high altar at that precise moment, a can of paint in one hand and a brush in the other, busy painting the back wall. I threw everything down on impulse, ran to Monsignor Kelly's room, and blurted out the words that had long been on my tongue, 'I want to be a priest.'[6]

The rector didn't seem to be a bit surprised. Nellie would have already told him of her brother's interest in the priesthood and of his setbacks and disappointments. Monsignor Kelly advised Pat to enrol immediately in St

Thomas' Christian Brothers school, to begin his secondary education, and promised to take care of the school fees. He was six feet four inches tall, and approaching twenty years of age, when he joined a class of thirteen- and fourteen-year-old boys in St Thomas'. When his brother Tom also expressed an interest in priesthood Monsignor Kelly generously volunteered to sponsor his education too. They applied themselves rigorously to their studies and made rapid progress. Seven years later, they both graduated from Notre Dame University, in Pat's case *magna cum laude*.

Pat first encountered Holy Cross priests in the spring of 1929 while they were conducting a parish mission in Scranton cathedral. He was impressed by their preaching and their joyfulness. The Holy Cross Congregation of priests and brothers was founded in 1837 by Blessed Basile Moreau at Sainte-Croix, near Le Mans in France, to work as educators of the faith; they were charged by their founder 'to make God known, loved, and served, and thus save souls'. Today, the Congregation of Holy Cross consists of over twelve hundred perpetually professed religious brothers and religious priests, serving in sixteen countries, including Ireland and the United States, where its most famous foundation is Notre Dame University in Indiana, a leading Catholic university in the USA.

Pat approached Fr Patrick Dolan CSC, the leader of the mission team in Scranton, and told him of his desire to become a priest. Father Dolan was supportive as was Monsignor Kelly, who gave him a glowing recommendation:

> In reference to Patrick Peyton's application as a candidate for the preparatory work for the priesthood, I unhesitatingly recommend him. He is gifted with excellent talent, he shows visible signs of a vocation, and is anxious for the spread of the Kingdom of God on earth … I shall consider any community or religious order or congregation or bishop quite fortunate to have his services.[7]

Members of the Holy Cross community took the traditional vows of poverty, chastity and obedience. In addition, the congregation also had its own well-defined characteristics, which appealed to Pat. Obedience, for Holy Cross members, did not imply 'blind obedience' but rather 'reasoned obedience'. He liked also that the congregation was open to helping the diocesan clergy, as one of its primary purposes, and that it adopted the family as its model of community. Members of the community were bound more by common aspirations, common experience, mutual affection and sharing in suffering than by the cold words of a contract.

Having finished the academic year at the Christian Brothers school in Scranton, on 29 August 1929, the Peyton brothers moved six hundred miles west to the University of Notre Dame in South Bend, Indiana to begin the high school seminary programme there. With their high school studies completed by 1932 and having taken temporary vows, they began a four-year academic programme for a Bachelor of Arts degree at the university. They looked on the course as another mountain they had to climb to become priests. Pat was a gifted student, who impressed his fellow students and his professors with his academic ability and his gentle nature.

Father Cornelius Hagerty CSC, who taught Pat metaphysics in Notre Dame, was impressed by him:

> His docility startled me. What I assigned, he studied carefully and earnestly; it seemed as if he committed it to memory; yet he could stand examination on its meaning. He never quarreled or disagreed with me; his attitude was that of an Irish country boy toward his schoolmaster who was also a priest.[8]

He was also noted for his remarkable memory. Years later, Fr Tom recalled, 'I had to study hard for everything I learned, but Pat had a phenomenal memory. He could hear a lecture and repeat it next day almost word for word. Or he could read something once in a book and remember it.'[9] Despite this, Fr Tom said, 'Pat pushed himself too far'. Though no one realised it as he came and went to classes, overwork was beginning to take its toll on the young seminarian.

Among his fellow seminarians at the time was Theodore M. Hesburgh CSC, who was, for thirty-five years, President of the University of Notre Dame. In his introduction to Fr Peyton's autobiography, Fr Hesburgh relates a story which illustrates Pat's compassion, dynamism and determination.

One day a horse belonging to the community strayed and Pat and a fellow student went to look for the animal. During the search they came upon a run-down area where the very poor lived in those dark days of the Great

Depression. Pat, of course, was immediately concerned about their faith and asked them what their religion was. Most of them said, 'Catholic'. He then asked, 'Do you come to Mass at Notre Dame?' Practically all of them said 'no', explaining that they didn't have decent clothing and were embarrassed to attend Sacred Heart Church at the university. They finally captured the horse, but Pat was troubled by the circumstances in which the poor people found themselves. He reasoned that if they couldn't come to Sacred Heart they ought to have a chapel of their own. The seminarians spent most of that summer building a church for them. The students chipped in with what little money they had to buy some cheap lumber from North Carolina. Many of the seminarians were pretty good carpenters and, before the summer was over, the church had been built. The people turned out in great numbers for the blessing and dedication on 15 August, the Feast of the Assumption. The new parish was called 'Little Flower' after St Thérèse of Lisieux. In conclusion Fr Hesburgh CSC declared, 'I found out then that you just could not beat Pat when he really wanted to do something good.'[10]

In 1934 their father, John Peyton, died at the age of sixty-six. He had been in poor health for over twenty years. They had exchanged letters regularly and prayed for one another constantly. John had been overjoyed when he received a photo of his two sons in their religious habits, as vowed religious. In reply he wrote: 'May God bless and spare ye to wear them right. Mother and I are filled with joy to see what God has done for our two boys.'[11] He bequeathed to his family, and especially to Pat, a deep-seated faith and a love of prayer that sustained them throughout their lives. It was this rich inheritance that inspired and enabled Pat to conduct an international ministry to promote family prayer and values.

Pat appreciated what he had inherited. 'God let me be born in a Rosary home ... In my childhood the family Rosary let me see every night my mother and father kneeling beside each other in adoration and love of God as they recited out loud the tremendous sentences of the Rosary'.[12] He never forgot the role his family played in his spiritual and personal development, and he never skipped an opportunity to acknowledge his family and express his gratitude to them. Father John Murphy CSC, who worked alongside Fr Peyton on the Rosary crusades, wrote to his sister Kitty, 'Fr Pat never forgot for a minute that he owes everything that he has ever accomplished to his wonderful family.'[13]

In October 1938 Pat began to feel unwell. He lacked energy and drive. He became alarmed when he began to spit up blood. In a matter of weeks, the spitting of blood became a full haemorrhage. He was sent to a specialist, Dr Malcolm Lent, who diagnosed him with 'advanced tuberculosis of the right upper lobe, with consolidation and a small cavity'.[14] He was immediately transferred to Providence Hospital, about a mile from Holy Cross College. There he spent three months, but, rather than responding to treatment, his condition grew progressively worse. In May 1939 he was transferred to the infirmary at Notre Dame from where he received further treatment at Healthwin Sanitarium in South Bend. However, his condition continued to deteriorate with little or no hope of recovery apparent.

He now entered a period of almost total desolation:

> Even prayer no longer brought me any happiness. In fact, it was an effort to pray at all. I would turn on the radio, but I soon got bored ... I could not concentrate on anything. So, I lay on the bed all through those burning summer months and stared at the ceiling day after day, week after week, month after month, knowing all the time that I was getting worse instead of better.[15]

Late in July of that year he was consoled on receiving a letter from his sister Nellie, announcing her forthcoming visit. Although they did not have the opportunity to see each other often, he had kept in regular contact with his family in Scranton, and especially with Nellie. At this juncture she was employed by Dr William J. Hafey, Bishop of Scranton, as his housekeeper, caring for him and the ten priests who resided with him. She was extremely happy in those surroundings, close to the cathedral, where she could attend Mass every morning and where she could frequently visit during the day, when she had a break from her duties. Pat felt strongly that he owed the fulfilment of his vocation to her more than to any other family member. He believed that she had committed her life in a special way to the furthering of Tom's and his progress toward priesthood. Nellie gave her brother several novena books and got him to promise to join her in novenas to the Blessed Virgin. Her extraordinary faith and her serenity raised his spirits. His illness was more bearable while she was around, and he dared to hope once again. Nellie returned to her duties in Scranton in September.

In October 1939 doctors offered Pat two basic options: surgery or prayer.

Medical science so far had not been successful; the two options provided were a last resort. While he was considering his lot, he had a visit from a former professor of his, Fr Cornelius Hagerty CSC. He challenged Pat to demonstrate anew his faith and confidence in God and Mary, by fighting for his life. Just as his own people in Ireland had always placed their trust in the Blessed Virgin, the mother of God, so should Pat do so, in his hour of greatest need.

Pat took Fr Hagerty's words to heart and abandoned all thoughts of surgery. He would instead place his trust in God, approaching him through Mary, his mother. Father Peyton relates in his autobiography the changes he observed in himself following his friend's visit:

> Father Hagerty's visit to me was about 25 October, and during the following days my peace of mind and confidence grew. I prayed constantly to Mary to cure me, and it was on Halloween, the eve of All Saints, that I knew she had decided to do just that. I was eating my supper in bed, and the radio was playing some Irish tunes, transmitted from London. Just then the oppression and the depression and the darkness were swept from my soul, to be replaced by lightness and freedom, and hope. I had been up and down many times, but this was different. The fog had finally lifted.[16]

By 31 October, Pat knew in his heart he had been cured. Two consecutive treatments at Healthwin Clinic verified that his lungs had been cleared; the effects of the tuberculosis were reversing themselves. The doctors had no scientific explanation for what had happened; they were cautious in their response and wanted the full six-month treatment to continue.

Pat pestered the Healthwin officials, however, who examined him completely on 15 January 1940. Finding no trace of tuberculosis, they released him from the infirmary and cleared him to resume classes at Holy Cross College. Pat was convinced that he had regained his health and strength through the intercession of Mary. He said, 'I'm giving witness to the power of Mary's intercession and the quiet, unsensational way she works.'[17]

During his convalescence he had received word that his mother was dying in Ireland. It was his brother Tom who broke the news of her death to him on 3 December 1939. Mary Peyton had suffered a stroke in July, but, aware of Pat's condition, she had prayed that his suffering would come upon her. A second stroke left her in great pain, but instead of complaining, she prayed for the health of her son.

Pat's sisters, Mary and Nellie, told him later that they were certain their mother would die instead of him. They believed that she had sacrificed herself for his benefit and that of the ministry he would conduct in the future. His family were overjoyed at his recovery and, like him, believed that it was a miracle. Pat returned to his studies with strict instructions to get plenty of rest and to avoid undue exertion. His brother Thomas ensured that he obeyed doctor's orders, watching over him like a hawk.

Pat and Tom were still mourning their mother's death when, in the spring of 1940, they received the devastating news of the sudden death in Scranton of their dear sister Nellie, at the age of thirty-five. She had undergone surgery and seemed to be making a good recovery, when she suffered a fatal heart attack. Afterwards, a slip of paper was found in a drawer in her room. It read:

> I, Nellie Peyton offer Thee, dear Lord, all my thoughts, words and actions of this day, and every day, and even life itself, for my two brothers Thomas Francis Peyton and Patrick Joseph Peyton, that if it be thy holy will that they become priests, that never in their priestly lives will they commit a mortal sin.[18]

It was her morning offering. 'Even life itself,' she had written. And God accepted her offering. The priest who anointed her and gave her Holy Communion asked if she had any message for her brothers. She said, 'Tell them that if it be God's holy will that they become priests, I pray that they will be true priests like Jesus Christ'.[19]

Nellie's family was consoled to learn that all who knew her held her in high regard. The local bishop, who presided at her funeral Mass, said, 'We all learned from this humble maid.'[20] A priest told the grieving family that, 'Every one of the priests loved her.'[21]

After the funeral, Pat realised more clearly than ever the important contribution Nellie had made and would continue to make to his own life. He felt that he was permanently obligated to her because of the vow she had voluntarily made and gladly fulfilled to give herself, even her life, for his spiritual and temporal welfare. He resolved, in return:

> to lead a life which, in its intensity of love for God and his blessed mother and in the totality of its concentration on the work of God, would not only justify my own existence but would leave a surplus to equal all the good Nellie would have radiated around her, had she lived the normal human span.[22]

Patrick Joseph Peyton and his brother Thomas Francis Peyton were ordained priests together in Sacred Heart Church at Notre Dame on 15 June 1941. Pat, who was side by side with his brother in the church, was instructed to remain seated during most of the long ceremony, to minimise the strain. Following his ordination by the laying on of hands, he found his past flashing before his eyes:

> Here was I, a farm boy from Mayo, a road worker, a general handyman ... an obstinate and often ungrateful son. Now I was being transformed into another Christ. I was being given power to make Christ present in the Christian community under the appearances of bread and wine. I was being authorised to forgive sin in his name, I was being commissioned to preach his word ... to pour the saving waters of Baptism ... to strengthen the dying for their final journey.[23]

Days later they both travelled back to Scranton to celebrate their first solemn Masses in the company of their family and friends. Father Tom was assigned by his religious superiors to parish work, in New Orleans, while Fr Pat went back to Holy Cross College, Washington for a further year of theology.

CHAPTER 3

PROMOTING THE FAMILY ROSARY

Uppermost in Fr Peyton's mind, was how he might adequately express his gratitude to God and the Virgin Mary for his healing. He was like the psalmist who cried out, 'How can I repay the Lord for his goodness to me?' (Ps 116:12). His first proposal was that a large statue of the Blessed Virgin be erected on the lawn in front of the college in full view of the road, at a point where the lights of the cars would illuminate it at night. He canvassed his fellow students with a view to raising funds. His proposal, however, was rejected by his superior.

At this time Americans were transfixed as they followed the course of World War II, which had begun in Europe in 1939 and now spread to Africa, Asia and the Pacific. Just six months after the ordinations the USA was drawn into the conflict, following the attack on Pearl Harbour by the Japanese, on the morning of 7 December 1941. The terrible loss of life grieved Fr Peyton very much and he considered carefully what his own response should be to the war. He had read about Lepanto, the great battle in the Mediterranean Sea in 1571, when a Christian fleet had stopped Ottoman forces as they advanced on Rome, the very heart of Christendom, and how the Christian soldiers and sailors had knelt and prayed the Rosary before committing themselves to battle. In gratitude for the victory at Lepanto, Pope Pius V had proclaimed 7 October as the Feast of the Most Holy Rosary for the universal Church. Father Peyton felt strongly that the Rosary could play a part again in the victory of justice and the restoration of peace in the world. He visualised enrolling vast numbers of people in a new crusade:

> My mind ran forward with the idea. I would enlist in a great Crusade for the family Rosary not only the seventy men with whom I lived, but all the millions of servicemen, like the soldiers and sailors before the battle of Lepanto: and not only the servicemen, but their mothers and fathers and brothers and sisters, every family in the United States, every family in the world, all just giving ten minutes a day to recite the same prayer as the men of Lepanto, a prayer drawn from the Scriptures, breathing the inspired word of God.[1]

During a day of recollection in the seminary, on the last Sunday in January 1942, Fr Peyton decided on his course of action. He resolved that he would devote his whole life, his every effort, to promoting the daily recitation of the Rosary in the family home, just as his own family had done in their home in Carracastle. The crusade he was planning would, he believed, help to bring about peace in the world and an end to the war. It would also engender peace in the heart and peace in the home.

In a sermon preached a few years later he explained:

> In January 1942, a few months after my ordination, on a Sunday morning in Holy Cross College in Washington, I made a resolution that amounts to this – to spend myself until death to bring the family Rosary back to ten million homes, in America, and not to one less than that – and to bring the family Rosary back to home life, not for the month of May or October or Lent, but for always ...[2]

There was concern among many at that time that family life was under threat in the USA and that the family unit was breaking down. Father Edgar Schmeidler OSB, founder of the Family Life Bureau believed so and advocated change:

> That our family life is showing alarming symptoms of disease and unmistakable signs of decay is apparent to all who care to see ... There is every reason, therefore, to speak of conserving the family. It is high time for action on behalf of the home. Such action to be really effective will have to seek the causes of the family's troubles and apply the remedies there.[3]

The American hierarchy supported Schmiedler and in 1949 issued a statement entitled 'The Christian Family', calling the family crisis a present danger more fearsome than the atomic bomb.

Father Peyton believed that family prayer was the answer to the family crisis. In a 1946 radio talk he declared:

> I do not hesitate to say that home life – to become wholesome and strong and vigorous – must have daily family prayer as part of its very life, and one of the reasons for the sad fact of dying homes in our age is that we threw out daily family prayer and it must come back again if we want to save our home life.[4]

Father Peyton began his crusade with a letter to Bishop Edwin O'Hara of Kansas City, who had recently given a talk to the Holy Cross seminarians, telling him of his intention to promote the family Rosary. His response was enthusiastic beyond all expectation. He received a further endorsement from Bishop John F. O'Hara CSC, chief chaplain to the American Forces, and a former president of Notre Dame, who said:

> You have a wonderful idea. I will order all the chaplains in our armed forces to preach the family Rosary on four consecutive Sundays, and I will ask them to urge the servicemen to write home and urge their families to say the Rosary for their safety, for as long as they are in service.[5]

He had scarcely received these ringing endorsements when he was notified by his religious superior of his appointment as chaplain in Albany, New York, to Holy Cross Brothers at the Vincentian Institute, a high school for boys. They shared a building with a high school for girls, conducted by the Sisters of Mercy. Because he was still a convalescent, and under doctor's orders to take things easy, his duties were not onerous. Fortunately, as a result, he had time to continue with his own special mission. He was joined in that endeavour by Fr Francis Woods, of the Diocese of Albany, who would serve from 1943 to his death in 1964 as a close confidant and full partner in the mission of the Family Rosary Crusade. Together with Sr Magdalena, a Sister of Mercy at the Vincentian Institute, they planned a massive letter campaign to promote the Rosary.

Continuing his custom of conducting important business on Marian feasts, on 21 November 1942, the Feast of the Presentation of Mary, Fr Peyton sent a letter to all US bishops about his proposed programme. This posting was followed on 8 December with a similar appeal for support to all presidents of national lay organisations. A third letter, soliciting the assistance of twelve thousand six hundred parish priests in the country, was sent on 11 February. The letters were prepared by the women students at the Vincentian Institute and novices of the Mercy Sisters. A typical letter read in part:

> Fellow priest, then make this cause [family prayer] your own. Let your zeal and your love for God and Mary inspire the methods that you will use to assure success. Let us leave no stone unturned in our efforts to drive from the homes of our people the spirit of the world and to make way for the spirit of Mary. Raise your voice for the family Rosary and let this increase and make more effective that army of bishops, priests and religious, and lay persons to make America, the land of Our Lady, also the home of the family Rosary.[6]

The enthusiastic response to his letters prompted him to move his campaign to its next phase. He posted information leaflets and pledge cards to the bishops who responded, asking them to recruit families as 'family Rosary families'. Through his letter writing campaign he also gained the support of the major lay-led Catholic societies. The Catholic press also strongly supported his initiative, with many favourable editorials appearing in leading publications. *America* magazine, for example, offered a plug for family prayer: 'The family that prays in common is the family that loves in common.' His Holy Cross superiors were very impressed by the rapid progress this young priest was making and gave their wholehearted support to his efforts. His provincial, Fr Steiner CSC, wrote, 'May God bless your efforts, and may our Blessed Mother come to your aid in promoting this excellent fruitful practice.'[7]

Father Woods witnessed Fr Peyton's great zeal close-up:

> Father Peyton works with never a moment's lull, as though all depended on him, as though the minutes and hours of life ahead would never be sufficient to pay the debt. And work it is! Many a time I would be deeply affected and even concerned to see how tireless Fr Peyton works.[8]

CHAPTER 4

FAMILY THEATER
OF THE AIR

In the autumn of 1943, Fr Peyton used radio for the first time to promote family prayer. It was Fr Francis Woods who had secured a fifteen-minute weekly slot on Albany's WABY radio station for the recitation of the Rosary. There was such an enthusiastic response from listeners that the programme was later expanded to thirty minutes with music and short meditations added, before and after each mystery. Encouraged by the success of the weekly broadcasts in Albany, Fr Peyton aimed for a national broadcast – coast to coast – of the family Rosary.

After much persistence Fr Peyton persuaded Mutual Broadcasting Company in New York, and their director of religious programmes Elsie Dick – of the Jewish faith – to make a half hour slot available, free of charge, for the national broadcast on Mother's Day, 13 May 1945. By coincidence, that was the very day that President Harry Truman had set aside as a day of national thanksgiving, following the victory of Allied Forces in Europe. Father Peyton was now challenged to put together a quality programme that would be well received by the listeners. He made arrangements for the event to take place in the Guild Theatre on 52nd Street, hosted by New York's Archbishop Francis Spellman, who described Fr Peyton as the 'American Apostle of the Family Rosary'. The Sullivan family of Waterloo, Iowa, who had lost five sons when the USS *Juneau* sank in the Pacific Ocean during the war, agreed to lead the Rosary. The Blessed Sacrament Church choir promised to sing hymns between the mysteries. The special event was so widely advertised that a vast listenership was anticipated.

During a preparatory meeting someone, half seriously, suggested that Bing Crosby be requested to participate in the broadcast. On Good Friday, 20 April, Fr Peyton took up the telephone and told the operator, 'I'd like to speak to Mr Bing Crosby in Hollywood, California.'[1] He was informed that the star was away for the weekend. On Easter Monday, he called again only to be told that Bing was on set filming *The Bells of St Mary's,* in which, as it happened, he played a priest who tries to save a school from closure with help from Ingrid Bergman's Sister Superior. Father Peyton left his number, and, sure enough, Bing called him back. When he told Bing of his efforts to put the family Rosary back in the home and of the upcoming national broadcast, Bing simply said, 'You have me'. He was true to his word. He did speak at the end of the broadcast on a special link from California, as follows:

> I want my children to pray in our home, as well as in our church. That is why I want them to believe, as I believe, in the true glory and the true greatness and true significance of the family Rosary. In our home we believe in the family Rosary as a great force working for good, working for good against evil. We believe that today, as never before, this vital

force for good is necessary if we are to fashion from the holocaust of war the framework of lasting peace. As Christians, as Americans, we believe in the power and the necessity of family prayer in all homes. As Catholics, we believe the family Rosary to be the perfect family prayer.[2]

The broadcast was an enormous success. The programme had been transmitted by at least three hundred radio stations nationwide. The newspapers on the following day were laudatory in their reviews, describing the Rosary recited by the Sullivan family of Iowa as the most touching of all the VE Day (Victory in Europe Day) programmes. Elsie Dick always insisted that it was the best religious programme ever made for radio.

The national Rosary crusade, from small beginnings, was now firmly established. The farmer's son from Carracastle, who had battled successfully with poverty, a poor education and a life-threatening illness had, in less than three years, launched an independent apostolate to promote family prayer through the Rosary, culminating in a national radio broadcast. With the help of numerous volunteers, he had conducted a massive letter-writing campaign, reaching out to every diocese and parish in the land.

On 14 May, the day after the Mother's Day Broadcast, Fr Peyton visited the Diocese of Pittsburgh, where he addressed all the priests, at the invitation of Bishop Hugh Charles Boyle. Many of the pastors reacted favourably to his talk and invited him to preach a triduum (three days of prayer) in their respective parishes, in an effort to promote devotion to Our Lady and encourage the practice of the family Rosary.

The preaching of triduums, however, also helped to generate much needed funds to meet expenses already incurred and for the ongoing campaign. At the invitation of the pastor, Fr Peyton would arrive in a parish on a Saturday night, preach at all the Masses on Sunday, announcing that he would be preaching again on Sunday night and Monday night and winding up the triduum with a holy hour on Tuesday evenings. At this final service a collection would be taken up for the benefit of the Family Rosary Crusade. In this way, he raised some money while promoting his primary objective. He never appealed for money on radio or, in later years, on television.

Father Peyton also received financial support through Fritz Wilson of Pittsburgh, an admirer of Fr Peyton's work, who began a fundraising operation which helped his ministry significantly for many years. Wilson got a group of his friends and business associates to attend an annual luncheon, and each time he ended up with a substantial cheque for the Family Rosary Crusade. Similar support groups sprang up in Syracuse, Rochester and other cities in Upstate New York. He also received outstanding support from cities in Illinois, Pennsylvania, Florida, Ohio, Kansas and California.

Meanwhile, in October 1945, Fr Peyton's provincial, Fr Steiner CSC, assigned Fr Jerome Lawyer CSC, to assist Peyton in his ministry full-time. Father Lawyer had been ordained in 1939 and was assigned to Dhaka in Bangladesh, formerly East Pakistan. En route to his mission, he and five other Holy Cross religious were captured and imprisoned by the Japanese. He was finally released from the prisoner-of-war camp in February 1945, suffering from malnutrition and post traumatic stress. In a letter to Fr Lawyer, Fr Steiner speaks prophetically of Fr Peyton and his mission.

He wrote:

> Father Peyton has something in the Family Rosary ... We are convinced he has a mission that is going to succeed, and that our country, and even the world is going to profit. Father Peyton himself is a living saint. His simplicity impresses everyone ... Several incidents in Fr Peyton's life and work during this past year give evidence of supernatural interventions.[3]

Father Lawyer assisted Fr Peyton for sixteen years and became one of the main architects of the crusade.

Father Steiner, his immediate superior, was most anxious about Fr Peyton's health and continued to urge him not to over exert himself:

> Quite naturally I am always concerned about your physical condition. You must try and take the daily rest period as prescribed for you several years ago. Every six months or so you should get another check-up. Above all do not over-exert yourself. Zeal is a wonderful and commendable virtue, but we have a duty to look after our physical well-being. You are doing grand and fruitful work for our Blessed Mother but if you do not keep physically fit your activities will soon be curtailed.[4]

Father Peyton was grateful for Steiner's paternal concern. His new ambition was to have a weekly syndicated radio programme that would promulgate his message to the nation and beyond. For this he would require the cooperation of a radio network, from whom he would be seeking free airtime. He was advised that, to be successful, it would be useful to have a high-profile Hollywood personality featured in every episode. As Bing Crosby's participation had contributed greatly to the success of the initial nationwide broadcast, so might other stars draw the public's attention to the new weekly series Fr Peyton had in mind.

Brimming with confidence, he set out for Hollywood in July 1945, seeking the support of suitable celebrities to fit the bill. Yet, as he neared Los Angeles, he was assailed by doubts. Would anyone be interested in his proposal? Was his journey out west pointless, foolhardy even? Later, he admitted: 'All I had was faith, and it was surely being put to the test. I prayed and forced myself blindly ahead.'[5]

His first stop in Los Angeles was the cathedral, where he met a priest from the Diocese of Achonry in Ireland – his own home diocese – Monsignor John J. Cawley, vicar general, and a native of Gurteen, Co. Sligo. He, in turn, introduced Fr Peyton to Archbishop Cantwell who promised him the fullest cooperation. Father Peyton also met with Colonel Tom Lewis, founder and first head of Armed Forces Radio, later a lay auditor at the Second Vatican Council, and his famous actress wife Loretta Young. Both were willing to support Fr Peyton's dream. Through the good offices of Monsignor Cawley it was arranged that he would preach at Masses at the Good Shepherd Church,

Beverly Hills, which many of Hollywood's top celebrities attended. Here Fr Peyton met Irene Dunne, Charles Boyer, Maureen O'Sullivan, Ethel Barrymore and several other celebrities, all of whom agreed to assist him. Later he managed to secure support from many more stars, including Bing Crosby, Gregory Peck, Don Ameche, Shirley Temple, Maureen O'Hara and Jane Wyatt.

Father Peyton made a deep impression on the stars he met. His humility, shyness and spirituality won them over. The actress Jane Wyatt commented, 'He certainly hypnotised everyone in the congregation ... Somehow when Fr Peyton asked you for something, there was no way to say no!'[6] Ann Blyth, who was active in Fr Peyton's early Hollywood productions, said: 'I think that it didn't matter what faith or non-faith any of the stars had. They were all taken with him. He had a way of enchanting even those who perhaps didn't believe.'[7] Father Peyton's special qualities were not lost on journalists either. One wrote of him: 'To meet him personally is to know a man of God. Sincerity shines forth from him, and his simple faith in the value of prayer is an inspiring thing ...'[8]

By the end of August Fr Peyton felt that he had sufficient support from a group of stars and producers and all that was now required was free air-time for the broadcasts. His trip to Hollywood had been very successful and he was confident that he could negotiate a fair deal with the New York based networks. After many failed attempts, however, he accepted, with some regret, an offer from the Mutual Broadcasting System, New York. The agreement specified that Fr Peyton would supply a first-class programme, the content of which would be non-sectarian in nature; each programme would feature a major Hollywood star and he would be responsible for all production costs, including orchestra and writers. Father Peyton was particularly unhappy that he was not permitted to say the Rosary on air as part of the presentation. There was nothing sectarian about the concept of family prayer, however, so he could not be prevented from advocating that practice.

The format they eventually adopted, under the banner of 'Family Theater of the Air,' was that of a radio 'soap opera', with short and simple comments inserted into dramatic plots to sell the idea of family prayer. Al Scalpone, a Hollywood public relations agent, was responsible for the 'commercials', the two most famous being 'The family that prays together stays together,' and 'A world at prayer is a world at peace'.

Alfred Lord Tennyson's famous comment, 'More things are wrought by prayer than this world dreams of', was another popular 'commercial' motto. Catholic periodicals carried press releases proclaiming that Family Theater's purpose 'is to sell Daily Family Prayer to America as a basic help to a richer life at home, at work, at play, and to make the daily family Rosary an evening sacrifice in every Catholic home'.[9]

It was the custom at Holy Cross to allow its young priests to have a vacation with their families immediately after ordination, but wartime conditions had prevented the Peyton brothers from availing of that trip. In the summer of 1946, however, it was agreed that they should holiday in Ireland for three months, departing from New York on 27 July aboard the SS Washington, and arriving at Cobh, Co. Cork, on 2 August. And so, Tom and Pat returned to the Mayo village from which they had followed Mary, Beatrice and Nellie to America eighteen years before.

The only family members still living in Carracastle were Michael, the oldest of the family, and Annie Kate, the youngest. Soon after their arrival, the two priests with their brother and sisters knelt at their parents' grave in Killeen Cemetery, a short distance from Attymass parish church. They were naturally saddened that their parents were no longer there to welcome them or to converse with them around the turf fire. Nevertheless, they enjoyed their visit to their birthplace. Later, they visited their sister Sara and her husband in Strokestown, Co. Roscommon.

Father Woods and Fr Peyton spent a considerable part of their time in Ireland contacting priests and lay people who might advise and help them with their plans. In Dublin they met Frank Duff, founder of the Legion of Mary, who approved of their intentions and offered them the prayerful support of the legionaries. They also visited Knock Shrine in Co. Mayo where the Blessed Virgin, alongside St Joseph, St John and the Lamb of God, had appeared in August 1879. Father Peyton was pleased to preach there on 15 August, the Feast of the Assumption. After less than six weeks, both priests cut short their vacation to return to the USA to resume their preparations for the launch of Family Theater of the Air.

The Family Theater of the Air debuted on 13 February 1947 with *Flight from Home*, starring Loretta Young and Don Ameche and narrated by James Stewart. It was dedicated to the family 'with the hope that families everywhere will always be together and that your home will be a happy one – with the conviction that prayer, simple prayer, will keep it that way.'[10] The reaction to the first programme was highly favourable, though some Catholic listeners expressed disappointment that the broadcast did not include the recitation of the Rosary.

The weekly programme went from strength to strength. Father Jerome Lawyer reported to his superior general that:

> The Family Theater series of weekly broadcasts from Hollywood have been a great triumph. The letters from people all over the United States have proven to us that through this most beautiful programme on family prayer they have come closer to God and have already begun the Family Rosary in their homes.[11]

Edgar Kobak, president of the Mutual Broadcasting System, was so pleased with the productions that in August he extended the free air-time indefinitely and began to consider special half or full-hour programmes for Christmas and special holidays. By July 1947 the Family Theater of the Air was being carried by three hundred Mutual stations in the United States, sixteen shortwave stations directed across the Atlantic and Pacific, and Armed Forces Radio.

In addition to the stars who enlisted during his summer visit to Hollywood in 1945, Fr Peyton obtained the services of a vast array of other actors and other American personalities, including Walter Brennan, Van Heflin, Ozzie

& Harriet Nelson, Vincent Price, William Holden, Robert Young, Roddy McDowall, Bob Hope, Ronald Reagan, Donna Reed, Alan Young, Barbara Stanwyck, Jack Benny, Peter Lawford, and Richard Basehart as feature stars. In addition, programme hosts included Dana Andrews, Edward G. Robinson, Gary Cooper, Jack Haley, Nelson Eddy, Cesar Romero, Fred MacMurray, Ricardo Montalbán, Ray Milland, and Notre Dame football coach Frank Leahy.

While Family Theater was a team effort, it was clear to all that it was the personality, drive and complete dedication of Fr Peyton that kept the organisation focused and united. Peyton's central role was noted by the Vatican newspaper, *L'Osservatore Romano*:

> The merit of these first broadcasts is to be attributed to the tenacious will of the priest who, in his deep devotion to God and His Virgin Mother, found the strength to overcome discouragement which would have fallen upon anyone who would have had to face so many difficulties and setbacks.[12]

> He is literally a salesman of Our Lady, bearing humiliations and labours, living out of a suitcase, travelling by land and air. No sacrifice is considered too great; no demand too trivial when there is an opportunity to preach and work for the restoration of the daily family Rosary in every home.[13]

The Family Theater of the Air's radio broadcasts achieved great success and recognition and were the recipient of many awards, including the Thomas Edison Award and

American Legion Award. *Time* magazine called the series outstanding, and Radio Daily selected it as Mutual's best of the year. Father Peyton did manage to include the Rosary in the special editions for Mother's Day, Christmas and Easter.

Over a ten-year period, from 1947 to 1957, the Family Theater broadcast four hundred and sixty-two original half-hour programmes of contemporary drama that preached the message of family prayer. Truly a record to be proud of. However, the times were changing and the 1950s saw a rapid shift from radio to television as the principal entertainment medium. Accordingly, Fr Peyton began to concentrate on the new format with a view to deploying it to promote family prayer.

In May 1949 the Family Theater produced its first film for television, a twenty-minute short entitled *The Road to Peace,* starring Bing Crosby and Ann Blyth. The film depicted the evils of the world and suggested that they could be solved, in part, through daily prayer. Peyton's first hour-long film, however, was a star-studded one entitled *The Triumphant Hour* and told the story of the death and Resurrection of Christ. Celebrities Pat O'Brien, Maureen O'Sullivan, Jane Wyatt, Don Ameche, Roddy McDowall, the Bob Hope family, Morton Downey, Pedro de Cordoba, and Jack Haley all appeared. The programme was carried by NBC, CBS and ABC. The total audience was estimated at sixteen million. *The Boston Post* newsletter described it as, 'one of the most inspiring observances of Easter ever presented.'[14]

Encouraged by the success of their first hour-long film, they planned a second – *The Joyful Hour* – for release the following Christmas, featuring Ruth Hussey, Nelson Leigh, Lloyd Corrigan and Pat O'Brien and his family. Again, the response was overwhelming, with *The New York Times* saying, 'It combines a rare spiritual beauty with the broad appeal of fine theatre.'[15]

One of Fr Peyton's most popular films was *Hill Number One*, produced in 1951, which depicted the story of Golgotha and the Resurrection, as told by an army chaplain on the battlefield in Korea, to a disgruntled artillery crew hurling shells at an enemy hill. As the chaplain speaks of Good Friday and Easter Sunday the scene shifts to Jerusalem. When the action returns to Korea the chaplain exhorts the soldiers to trust Mary and pray the Rosary. This film starred Ruth Hussey, Joan Leslie, Leif Erickson, Jeanne Cagney, Gene Lockhart, and featured a brief appearance from a then unknown James Dean as St John the Apostle. The production received rave reviews; *The New York Times* described it as, 'one of the most nearly perfect performances ever seen on TV, mixing dramatic import with compelling simplicity.' The film was shown on one hundred and two television stations and the total audience was estimated at forty-two million.

The reaction to Fr Peyton's films was generally very positive. The chief critic at *The New York Times*, Jack Gould, extolled Fr Peyton and his work:

> The leading producer in this field is the Rev. Patrick Peyton, a Catholic priest of Hollywood, who has made a number of superb religious films with top-flight motion picture stars. He almost alone has seemed to recognise that with mass media the mode

of presentation is every bit as important as the message.[16]

But, compared to his radio endeavours, the costs involved in film production were staggering. It was clear that Fr Peyton's ministry could not continue without some major financial base from which to operate. The key to investment for the Family Rosary Crusade was centred around J. Peter Grace, whom Peyton had met in the summer of 1946. Their friendship was to last until the priest's death in 1992. At the time of their meeting Grace has just become president of W. R. Grace and Company, the multimillion-dollar international corporation started by his great-grandfather in 1854. The company made its name in shipping, with special interest in Latin American operations.

Grace greatly appreciated the work Fr Peyton was doing. 'It has been a great thrill to have any part in the Family Rosary Crusade [which] … seems to me to be the only answer to the situation in which we find ourselves today.'[17] Grace worked with Fr Peyton to create a long-term financial plan for all the Family Rosary operations. He believed that Peyton's great contribution to Family Rosary was his spiritual guidance, not his financial development efforts. He wrote:

> Fr Peyton has reached what appears to be the end of his development road for no other reason than a financial obstacle. It seems to us imperative that this famed apostle of Christ be permitted not only full time on the spiritual work required but also that the

> financial worries which are so handicapping any attempt to plan for the future, be taken away from Fr Peyton and his associates.[18]

Father Peyton was happy to entrust all the major financial decisions of the organisation to Grace.

Despite the financial constraints, Fr Peyton's two-fold ministry – on radio and television – had prospered beyond all expectations. Friends and colleagues were encouraging and urged him on to still greater achievements. Al Scalpone, a marketing executive for the media said: 'With radio and television you can accomplish – nay *are* accomplishing – the objective of the crusade on a scale never dreamed possible before the age of electronics.'[19]

Thomas O'Neill, chairman of the board of Mutual Broadcasting System, also praised Fr Peyton's accomplishments:

> I am ... privileged to join with your many other friends at this time in paying to you my sincere and everlasting tribute for your stimulating and inspirational work in bringing to millions your theme, 'the family that prays together, stays together.' It is our cherished hope that for many years to come it may be our privilege and pleasure to participate with you in bringing to millions of American families these now nationally known and worthwhile programmes.[20]

Still greater challenges and achievements lay ahead.

CHAPTER 5

BIRTH OF THE
ROSARY CRUSADE

Fathers Peyton, Woods and Lawyer attended an International Marian Congress in Ottawa, in the Autumn of 1947, to publicise the Family Theater of the Air and explain its objectives. It was while they were in conversation with Fr John T. Maloney, from the Diocese of London, Ontario that the idea of a Rosary Crusade was first conceived.

Father Maloney told them of a very successful fundraising drive in his home diocese that had raised several million dollars to fund the building of hospitals and schools. The professional fundraisers' technique involved motivation and organisation. Congregations had been addressed in their churches and afterwards volunteers visited every Catholic home in the diocese to obtain a pledge for a certain amount. 'Why,' asked Fr Maloney, 'don't we use the same technique to obtain a pledge, not of money, but of the daily recitation of the Rosary, in every family?'[1]

After consultation with Bishop John T. Kidd, plans for a diocesan-wide crusade were formulated. The bishop wrote a pastoral letter to the people explaining the crusade and encouraging them to support it. It was also decided that during the five weeks of the crusade a weekly newspaper, *The Time for Family Prayer*, would be circulated. This publication, which became a feature of all subsequent crusades, contained news of the crusade as well as articles of interest by Hollywood celebrities and other well-known individuals. Actresses Loretta Young and Louella Parsons contributed regularly, as did Claire Booth Luce, writer, politician and USA ambassador.

The most crucial part of the crusade, the one to which all other efforts were directed, was the pledge drive conducted during the final week. The crusade pledge was: 'To obtain peace for the nations of the world and the love and protection of God and Mary for myself and the members of my family, I promise to recite the daily Family Rosary.'[2] Pledge workers also asked the aged and infirm to pray for the crusade's success.

In the Diocese of London, Ontario seven thousand men volunteered to go from door to door with the pledges. In the second edition of the crusade paper Cardinal Francis Spellman of New York wrote:

> In this hour of world crisis, the Crusade for Family Prayer with the Rosary in your diocese is most edifying, helpful and urgent. The spirit of prayer can bring peace on earth. Family Prayer is one of the surest means of keeping the family, both of individuals and nations, holy and united. Indeed, the family that prays together stays together. Those nations that pray together will never go to war. May our Lady of the Rosary intercede at the Throne of Mercy for the world to win a triumph for Christianity over Godless Communism by the power of prayer.[3]

As part of the programme Fr Maloney arranged for Fr Peyton to speak at two diocesan clergy conferences to inform and enthuse the priests. He also preached in each parish of the diocese, speaking in three parishes every day, an extremely taxing programme indeed. His homilies always included his personal testimony:

> It is my personal testimony, my witness, my proclamation of the great things that Mary had done to me, her unworthy servant … the family love engendered and fostered by family prayer to the point that my mother and my sister were happy to give their lives so that I might live and perform my assigned task of proclaiming all over the earth the greatness of God and the sensitive love his Mother has for every one of Christ's brothers and sisters, her children.[4]

Peyton's preaching was always compelling; when he spoke, there was a stillness that was to be experienced rather than described. He held his listeners spellbound:

> But when I get on the platform or in the pulpit I join with my listeners in reciting a Hail Mary for guidance … I am not there to seek for myself but only for her. My function is not to impress them with my oratory but to proclaim to them my experience, to have them understand the great things Mary has done to me and for me. And while what I say is always the same, in another sense it is new each time. It is like the devoutly recited Hail

Mary, always the same greeting, yet constantly renewed by the spirit with which it is said.[5]

Peyton became a naturalised American citizen in 1938, but, of course he remained a proud Irishman to the end. He never lost his lilting west of Ireland brogue. He also never forgot the role his family played in his spiritual and personal development. His Irish heritage imbued him with the belief that the family was the bedrock of society and faith, and that its restoration to a place of prominence in contemporary life was essential. Peyton observed a worrying tendency in society towards making the home merely a place for eating and sleeping.

The London Crusade was a great success. It was not long before Archbishop Michael O'Neill of the Archdiocese of Regina expressed interest in a similar event. He invited all the bishops of the province of Saskatchewan to a meeting with Fr Peyton and Fr Woods. It was agreed that in the interests of efficiency the preparatory work would be staggered. When Frs Wood and Finan had initiated the process in one diocese, they would move on the next.

Crusades usually ran for eleven weeks, the first five of which were preparation. Once Fr Peyton set dates with local bishops, a special team was sent to the city or town five weeks before the opening day. The team consisted of at least one priest and generally two lay secretaries. The priests were Francis Woods and/or John Murphy or later Joseph Quinn. The team set up the crusade office, arranged the rally sites, obtained advertising and drummed up support by sending literature to all parishes and schools. Press conferences were held to promote the crusade and meetings with the clergy were arranged. Father Peyton would attend the preliminary meetings, especially when opportunities arose to address fellow clergy. He relied heavily on the dedicated men and women of the front team who worked for twelve to fourteen hours a day to ensure the success of each crusade.

In addition to *The Time for Family Prayer,* the crusade newspaper, each campaign published its own Crusade Handbook, explaining procedures and providing general information. Handbooks were also printed and distributed for teachers, clergy, and pledge leaders. Parish kits containing posters, prayer cards, pledge cards and the necessary handbooks were sent to parishes before the crusade formally began.

The last part of the preparation was the responsibility of the local bishop. He appointed a local diocesan director to work with the Crusade team. The bishop then formally announced the Crusade through the publication of a pastoral letter which was read on one Sunday at all Masses. The work of the formal Crusade began with a series of dinner meetings where priests were told their important role in the campaign. Schools and teachers were also organised to promote the Crusade; the local bishop called meetings at which Fr Peyton would explain the purpose of the campaign, emphasising the teacher's specific role. Sunday sermons on family prayer and the family Rosary were made available to local clergy for use during the five or six weeks of the formal crusade.

The rally, which was generally held in a large stadium, park or public meeting place, was the highlight of each crusade. The aim was to bring as many people as possible together in one place for a grand demonstration of faith and a public commitment of the diocese to the service of God and Mary. Rallies were major events for the local communities and drew people from entire regions. The programme featured hymn singing, recitation of the Rosary, and addresses by local bishops and dignitaries, with Fr Peyton's passionate and stirring talk as the grand finale.

Peyton's charismatic presence at the rally was crucial to the success of the Crusade, but his time physically present during the actual five or six weeks of the campaign was rather limited, as Fr Joseph Quinn CSC, explains: 'He mostly talked at the rally. He would put all his efforts into that. He would help us at the beginning to get some people for publicity ... but he never took part in the physical preparations.'[6]

From Saskatchewan, news of the Crusade spread through all western Canada, leading to a meeting at Calgary, Alberta to discuss its extension to other dioceses. At least a dozen bishops attended, and others sent representatives. They came from British Columbia, Manitoba and Alaska, as well as from Alberta. The upshot of this meeting was that they blanketed the whole vast region of western Canada, all the way up to the Arctic Circle and beyond, to Hudson Bay, Whitehorse and Mackenzie, using all kinds of conveyances – from airplane to dog sled – and experiencing all kinds of weather-related setbacks that, for them, were totally new.

There was an established practice in the Holy Cross Congregation whereby members who felt a special call to the foreign missions would take an additional vow, committing them to any foreign mission the superior general might send them. When Peyton made his perpetual or final vows he included the fourth vow for the foreign mission. His brother Tom, preferring to minister in the United States, declined the fourth vow. Subsequently, because of Fr Peyton's ill-health he was strongly advised by his superiors not to pursue a life in the foreign missions. But now, new mission fields were opening up before him – new opportunities for him to pursue his 'assigned task of proclaiming all over the earth the greatness of God and the sensitive love his Mother has for every one of Christ's brothers and sisters, her children.'[7] With Pauline zeal, he was now undertaking missionary journeys of his own.

As they were flying to Calgary for the meeting, Fr Woods drew Fr Peyton's attention to a newspaper report about a plane crash in India, the pilot having flown the aircraft into the side of a mountain. Listed among the dead was their friend Elsie Dick, of the Mutual Broadcasting System in New York, who had approved the 1945 Mother's Day programme. They remembered her with gratitude, in a prayer.

Along with an understandable emphasis on Catholic prayers and traditions, from the outset Peyton's Crusades also fostered an ecumenical spirit, a rarity in the period. In Saskatchewan he stated: 'The main idea of the Family Rosary Crusade is to have all Catholics recite the Rosary daily in their homes; the secondary objective is to bring the people of all faiths to a realisation that prayer is absolutely necessary in these troubled times.'[8]

The Crusade made every effort to appeal and reach out to people of faith, regardless of denomination, even to non-Christians. The ecumenical message reached people, as evidenced by the presence of a not insignificant number of non-Catholics at rallies wherever the Crusade was held. 'Ministers of every creed have praised and supported Fr Peyton's work just as actors and musicians of differing beliefs have been unanimously generous in contributing their time and talent.'[9]

The ecumenical tone of the crusades was noted by a secular journalist in an editorial in the *Vancouver Sun* newspaper, under the title, 'With One Accord':

> The Family Rosary Crusade is sponsored by, but not limited to, the Roman Catholic Church. It makes its appeal to all who acknowledge the supremacy of God and believes that he works with and for those who put their trust in him, and whose homes he rules … For those to whom the invocation of the saints seems akin or false in doctrinal implications, the Family Crusade urges merely that *some* form of daily family devotion, such as could be wholeheartedly adopted in every devout Protestant or Jewish household, be restored or begun as a spiritual bulwark in these anxious and troubled times.[10]

The spirit of openness to non-Christians was subsequently very evident at rallies in the Far East, which were supported not only by Christians, but also by Hindus, Muslims, Sikhs and Parsis, all of whom recognised Peyton as a good and holy man. A secular newspaper, the *Nation*, in Burma (Myanmar) reported:

> Last week there came to Burma a good man, a holy man, a man of God. In a few days he was gone, and the manner of his going was as unobtrusive as his coming. But he left implanted in the minds of several thousand people a tiny seed, destined one day to grow into something reaching the very sky.[11]

News of the success of the Family Rosary Crusades in Canada spread throughout the United States. Bishop William Hafey of Scranton, Pennsylvania was the first American bishop to invite Peyton to conduct a Crusade in his diocese. Scranton was the only place in America which Peyton regarded as home, the place he had emigrated to in 1928. Bishop Hafey wrote to his diocese: 'It is our fervent hope that all ... families, recognising the desperate need in our times for a return to family prayer, will find the grace and courage to sign their daily Family Prayer pledge and keep it faithfully.'[12]

The Crusade, which took place between 16 October and 20 November 1949, featured five rallies, the largest of which drew fifty thousand people to Scranton.

Bishop Hafey was so pleased with the response in his diocese that he became a promoter of the Crusade among the neighbouring bishops. In October 1950 the Crusade moved to the archdioceses of Louisville and Indianapolis and their suffragan dioceses. In some ways it was another homecoming for Peyton, most especially on 22 October, when thirty-five thousand people poured into Notre

Dame football stadium to hear him speak. An even larger crowd – some fifty-two thousand – gathered for a rally in Indianapolis. From there Peyton took his campaign to Crookston, Minnesota between 15 October and 19 November 1950. Francis Wood made all the preparatory arrangements, while Peyton addressed fifteen thousand people at the one and only rally of the campaign.

The next Crusade, which took place from 30 September to 4 November 1951, covered nine archdioceses and dioceses along the mid-Atlantic coast from Baltimore to Atlanta. Francis Woods and John Murphy CSC made all the preparatory arrangements conveying information through eight local Catholic newspapers, including the *Catholic Standard* of Washington DC, the *Catholic Review* in Baltimore, the *Providence Visitor* and the *Bulletin,* published in the Diocese of Savannah-Atlanta. Peyton spoke at all eighteen rallies, addressing an audience of seventy thousand on 28 October in Washington. A grand total of two hundred and eighteen thousand attended the eighteen rallies.

In 1952 the crusade was conducted in the South, centred at New Orleans, and in the Archdiocese of New York. Archbishop Joseph Rummel of New Orleans hosted the crusade between 13 January and 17 February. Twenty rallies were held in cities of the Dioceses of Alexandria, Lafayette, Little Rock, Mobile and Natchez, with a crowd of one hundred and ten thousand at New Orleans on 3 February, setting a record for the Crusade. The attendance included the governors of Arkansas and Mississippi. The mayor of New Orleans declared 3 to 10 February as 'Family Prayer Week' in the city.

New York's Crusade took place from 14 September to 19 October 1952. Of the five rallies held, the most spectacular by far was the one at the Polo Grounds on 12 October, attended by seventy-six thousand. Cardinal Francis Spellman echoed Peyton's sentiments in his talk:

> For many years past the spirit of the world has been seeping into homes, dampening family spirit, disrupting family ties and destroying family virtues. The inevitable result is our nation is nearing the brink of disaster. For as the family goes, so goes the country. To restore and to preserve the integrity, the sanctity and the peace of our homes, and thus save our nation's life, it is the high duty that devolves upon us all, impelling us to be faithful in the daily recitation of the Family Rosary for these intentions. For it has been demonstrated that the family which prays together stays together, bound together by the holy ties of faith in Mary, hope in Mary and love for Mary.[13]

As international crusades predominated in the mid-1950s the US based ones were generally small. The Cleveland Crusade was held between 31 May and 5 July 1953. It was notable for the introduction of the fifteen mysteries of the Rosary radio broadcasts that were sponsored by Catholic Daughters of America. These radio shows became standard in American Crusades and later worldwide, after they were translated into Spanish. In October 1955 Fr Peyton received an invitation from Bishop Edwin O'Hara to hold a Crusade in Kansas City.

He was happy to accept, remembering that O'Hara had helped him launch his Family Rosary operation in 1942. The Crusade then moved to the Pacific Northwest first to the Diocese of Juneau, Alaska and then south to the Archdioceses of Seattle and Portland and their six suffragan dioceses.

Bishop James Byrne of Boise expressed his appreciation to the superior general of Holy Cross for Peyton and his work: 'I do not need to tell you, Fr O'Toole, how impressed I was by the sincerity and singleness of purpose of Fr Peyton ... Having the opportunity of watching him for the past five days that I was with him during the week, I could not help but feel that God is using him to do very important work.'[14]

The first international crusades outside Canada were a series of campaigns in England in 1951 and 1952. It was Bishop Thomas Flynn of Lancaster who first invited Fr Peyton to England to conduct a Crusade in his diocese, having met him in Lourdes in August 1949. The Lancaster crusade took place from 11 February to 11 March 1951 with Peyton speaking at six rallies in the region. Bishop Flynn was more than delighted with the response to his visit:

> I wish to say that his (Peyton's) visit to the diocese has been a stupendous success ... Everywhere he has inspired the greatest enthusiasm for the cause of the Family Rosary. Clergy and laity alike have taken him to their hearts and have responded with the utmost zeal to his appeal. I look for a great spiritual revolution in the diocese as a result of this man's

work. I am convinced that nothing greater has happened in my time.[15]

In his introduction to Fr Peyton's book *The Ear of God*, Bishop Flynn writes of '… his great-hearted simplicity, tireless energy, (and) deep personal humility … A giant of a man, he has the heart of a child, the simplicity, directness and sensitiveness of a child.'[16]

The next English Crusade took place in the Newcastle, Hexham and Middleborough region between 20 April and 25 May 1952. Bishop Joseph McCormick recommended Fr Peyton very highly to his people: 'In Father Peyton I have a priest who has devoted his life to this apostolic work. He has experience; he has understanding; he has the Holy Father's personal recommendation and blessing.'[17] Family Theater films were used extensively in parishes and schools. The crusade culminated with one hundred thousand in attendance at a rally in Newcastle.

The Archbishop of Birmingham hesitated at first to invite Peyton to his diocese but was very glad in the end that he did so. All fourteen rallies were successful, including one with an attendance of eighty-five thousand in Birkenhead on 1 June. When the Crusade ended the archbishop remarked: 'I thought he (Peyton) might be a high-powered American salesman such as I have seen in the cinema, but when I met him I found he was a very humble and holy man … I became one of his greatest admirers and I am delighted he has been able to come to this diocese.'[18]

The English campaign ended with the London crusade (Archdiocese of Westminster), beginning with one hundred thousand people attenting a rally in Hyde Park and concluding with a massive rally in Wembley Stadium attended by eighty-three thousand.

In a letter to His Eminence Cardinal Griffin, Archbishop of Westminster, on the Family Rosary Crusade in Wembley, London his holiness Pope Pius XII made the following appeal:

> Never before has the world been so direly in need of prayer as at the present time, when a dangerous form of materialism tends to undermine man's relations with his Creator and with his fellow man and to destroy the sanctity of family life.
>
> The most powerful antidote against the evils that threaten human society is prayer, especially collective prayer, for Our Divine One has said: 'If two of you shall consent upon earth concerning anything whatsoever they shall ask, it shall be done unto them by my Father who is in heaven. For where there are two or three gathered together in my name, there I am in the midst of them'. (Mt 28:19-20)
>
> And what form of collective prayer could be simpler and yet more efficacious than the Family Rosary, in which parents and children join in supplicating the Eternal Father, through the intercession of their most loving Mother, meditating meanwhile on the most sacred mysteries of our faith? There is no surer means of calling down God's Blessing upon the family and especially of preserving peace and happiness in the home, than

the daily recitation of the Rosary. And apart from its supplicatory power, the Family Rosary can have very far reaching effects, for, if the habit of this pious practice is inculcated into children at an impressionable age, they, too, will be faithful to the Rosary in later life and their faith will be nourished and strengthened …

We earnestly exhort those of our beloved children towards whom the Crusade has been directed to regard the joint recitation of the Rosary in the family circle as the most important collective act in their daily lives, and a most certain way of obtaining grace.[19]

Early in 1953, from 25 January to 28 February, Fr Peyton and his co-workers conducted a Crusade in Malaga in Spain, at the invitation of Bishop Angel Herrera. In preparation, Peyton had undertaken an intensive course in Spanish, learning the language well enough to speak at the rallies. An estimated total of one hundred thousand people attended the six rallies.

Peyton first visited Australia at the invitation of Irish-born Archbishop Daniel Mannix, of Melbourne, in November 1951, to speak at a special jubilee year celebration. He was warmly received on that occasion by a crowd of eighty thousand at an open-air event. He promised to return and did so in August 1953 to conduct a series of Rosary Crusades over a five-month period, covering twenty-six dioceses in Queensland, New South Wales and Melbourne. There were numerous rallies, the two largest being in Sydney with one hundred and ten thousand attendees and in Melbourne with one hundred and fifty thousand participants.

From Australia Fr Woods went to Papua New Guinea and held Crusades in the two apostolic vicariates, just before Christmas 1953. Afterwards, together with Fr Peyton they went south to New Zealand, in the first months of 1954. The Crusade, which encompassed the entire nation through its four dioceses, featured eleven rallies, with the best attended at Auckland (thirty-three thousand) and Wellington (twenty-five thousand). The next destination was Ireland. On 25 April, four days after completing the mission in New Zealand, Fr Peyton arrived in Tuam, Co. Galway, to begin a four-month campaign in his native land.

CHAPTER 6

THE IRISH CRUSADE

It was appropriate that Fr Peyton should visit Ireland during the Marian Year – the first in the history of the Church – a year of special devotion to Mary marking the centenary of the proclamation of the dogma of the Immaculate Conception. Hundreds of thousands of Romans lined the route of the papal cortege when Pius XII, in one of his rare appearances in the streets of Rome, went to the Basilica of St Mary Major to open the Marian Year on 8 December 1953.

The Marian Year was an international event, but apparently no other country embraced the idea with greater fervour than Ireland. Hundreds of roadside shrines and grottoes were constructed that year. Maurice O'Donnell, a statue maker from Cork, recalled that 1954 was a bonanza year for him: '... I was making so many at that time there was no time to dry them out before painting, so lots of statues in the shrines around the country are still unpainted. But that was in the Marian Year. The bottom has dropped out of the statues market since the Vatican Council ...'

Commemorative stamps were issued by the state and a near majority of girls born in the country that year were named Marian or Mary. On 16 May of the year, thirty thousand faithful marched through Dublin in a huge Marian Year procession, the city's greatest display of Catholic piety since the International Eucharistic Congress of 1932.

The Church's role in the Ireland of the 1950s was dominant; its influence was all pervasive. Church practice among all age groups and classes was virtually 100 per cent. Priests and nuns were numerous, and Masses became more frequent as the number of priests increased. The small town of Swinford in Co. Mayo had a minimum of five Masses celebrated daily, two in the parish church and one each in the convent, hospital and domestic economy school. On most mornings there was also one or more requiem high Masses for funerals or anniversaries, requiring the participation of at least three priests. As the liturgies were in Latin many of those attending prayed their Rosaries or novenas; religious practice was dominated by private prayer.

The Church's strict control over recreational activities was generally uncontested. Dances were not permitted during Lent and Advent and were never held on Saturdays, ensuring that there was no clash with confessions and preparations for Sunday Mass. Cinemas also remained closed on Saturdays for the same reason. Priests were patrons or presidents of almost every club and society based in their parishes. A strategy of fear was often employed by preachers, in a paternalistic fashion, especially at parish missions.

But there was a downside to this regime. It was a priest-dominated Church with clericalism and authoritarianism very evident, while the role of the laity was limited to one of praying, paying and obeying!

Members of the Irish hierarchy collectively had not extended an invitation to Fr Peyton to visit Ireland, but the bishops from the west of Ireland had done so, extending a warm welcome to a native son. It must have given him great pleasure and satisfaction to bring the Crusade to his own people. Addressing the crowds at the rallies, he put his listeners at their ease with his opening remarks: 'I am your neighbour, from the bogs of Mayo!'[1]

He recalled his departure from Ireland twenty-five years earlier, describing himself as 'a penniless and uneducated emigrant. At that time, I thought of myself and the place and people I was leaving, as poor and backward. I looked forward to the land of opportunity where I would make a fortune.'[2]

But now he was older and much wiser and realised that he owed his own people a debt of gratitude. He was grateful to God and to his community '… for having been raised in a family and society which worshipped God, and which expressed that worship in devotion to His Mother and faithfulness to the recitation of the family Rosary.'[3] Of course, he urged his listeners to remain faithful to the tradition of Family Prayer, which was of incalculable worth: 'I come to plead with you to hold fast to that tradition and pass it to your children, for your own sake, for their sake, and for the sake of the example that we Irish give to the world by our devotion to the mother of God.'[4]

It is estimated that Fr Peyton addressed over half a million people directly at rallies in ten dioceses, in twenty-one centres during his Irish campaign, beginning in Tuam on 25 April 1954. A banner spanning the entrance to the town bore the greeting, 'Welcome Father Peyton'. The youth who, at the age of nineteen, had left Ireland was being welcomed home as the celebrated and internationally renowned founder of the Family Rosary Crusade. He had travelled non-stop from New Zealand, where he had addressed a rally on the previous Sunday, to keep this appointment with the Archbishop of Tuam, Dr Walsh.

From early morning, people had been arriving from all over the archdiocese and hundreds of motor cars lined the roads approaching the town. Thousands of people – men, women and children – walked in procession to the rally in the GAA stadium, reciting the Rosary as they went. The vast throng included a party of two hundred people from the Aran Islands, who had travelled by boat to Galway that morning and had taken the train to Tuam.

An *Irish Independent* reporter recorded his impressions of Fr Peyton and his impact on the crowd that day: 'Fr Peyton is a tall burly man, as kindly as he is persuasive, convincing and impressive in his heart stirring advocacy of ... Family Prayer. He won a niche in the affections of the Irish people ... He brought tears to their eyes and joy to their hearts.'[5]

The next rally was held in Clifden, Co. Galway, where people from all parts of Connemara gathered to listen to the Rosary Priest. Bunting, with papal and national flags, bedecked the streets. The Archbishop of Tuam, Dr Walsh, inspected a guard of honour drawn from the ranks of the local, Irish-speaking FCA battalion. A group of men carried a statue of Our Lady shoulder high in procession to the altar in the centre of the town.

Knock Shrine was the venue for the third great Rosary Rally in the Archdiocese of Tuam on Sunday, 2 May. Father Peyton addressed an estimated crowd of eighteen thousand people, many of whom had travelled through the early hours of the morning from distant parts of the country. Remarkable scenes of devotion were witnessed that day at the shrine, as Fr Peyton urged the people to be faithful to the Family Rosary.

On the evening of Tuesday, 4 May, Fr Peyton visited Gort, Co. Galway where he spoke to a large crowd assembled in the town square. He was accompanied by Michael Browne, Bishop of Galway and was greeted on arrival by Father M.J. Fallon, Dean of Kilmacduagh, who announced that all two thousand five hundred households in the deanery had signed the Rosary pledge.

Still in the Diocese of Galway, Fr Peyton next visited the town of Ennistymon, Co. Clare, accompanied by Bishop Michael Browne, on Thursday 6 May, where he addressed six thousand people. When he was leaving with the bishop and a procession of priests, the people, who had listened in silence to his address, greeted him loudly and finally broke through the line of stewards to shake Fr Peyton's hand.

An immense throng of more than thirty thousand people crowded the stands and general enclosure of the racecourse in Ballybrit, for the Galway city rally on Sunday, 9 May. A cross-bearer with acolytes led an impressive procession including the mayor and members of Galway Corporation in their robes of office, members of the Galway Harbour Board, Galway County Council, professors and staff of University College Galway, a large gathering of the diocesan chapter, the secular clergy and members of the various orders, followed by Fr Peyton and the Bishop of Galway, Dr Browne. The procession wound its way slowly up the racecourse to Our Lady's Altar, which had been erected opposite the grandstand and close to the Mass Rock.

An equally large number of people – more than thirty thousand – gathered in Loughrea on Sunday, 16 May 1954 with Bishop Philbin and priests and religious of the Diocese of Clonfert, to pay tribute to Our Lady at a Rosary Crusade Rally. It was regarded as the biggest gathering in the town since the Liberator, Daniel O'Connell, held his repeal demonstration there in 1843. A fourteenth-century statue of Our Lady of Clonfert was borne at the head of the procession in Loughrea. The huge crowd made an impressive sight as it snaked its way in a great semicircle around the open-air altar from which the Bishop of Clonfert and Fr Peyton addressed the people. In his tribute to Fr Peyton, Bishop Philbin said: 'Father Peyton is a man who has travelled round the world carrying the torch of love of God and His Mother. Nobody who met him could say he didn't feel the better for it. Father Peyton did not come to us in any spirit of ostentation or display. If there was ever an unpretentious man, it was Fr Peyton.'[6]

The Diocese of Achonry, and the town of Ballaghaderreen, hosted the next Rosary Rally on Sunday, 23 May. Thousands of people, from many parts of the diocese, stood in the Market Square for over an hour to listen to Fr Peyton, despite the heavy rain. The rally brought one of the largest crowds ever to the town. The

Bishop, James Fergus, attended with members of the cathedral chapter, clergy of the diocese and members of the religious communities.

The Crusade then moved to the Diocese of Elphin and the county town of Roscommon where, on Thursday, 27 May 1954, 'the heavens opened, and the rain came down in torrents, yet not a single person thought of leaving until the rally ended.'[7] Disregarding the weather conditions, an estimated crowd of twenty thousand gathered in St Coman's Park to pray the Rosary and listen to Fr Peyton's address. A procession to the park was led by a group of acolytes, clad in red and white, followed by flag-bearers, Children of Mary, girls and boys from the diocesan schools, sodalities, hospital nurses, clergy and the general public.

On the following Sunday, 30 May, the sun shone warmly on a crowd of twenty thousand people at the rally in the Showgrounds in Sligo. Father Peyton was accompanied by the Bishop of Elphin, Dr Hanly, and was greeted by army buglers and an FCA Guard of Honour. Five hundred Children of Mary, in their blue cloaks, formed the letter 'M' around the statue of Our Lady. Those present heard a stirring appeal for devotion to the Rosary from Fr Peyton. The rally concluded with the recitation of the Rosary and the singing of hymns.

Father Peyton next focused his attention on the Diocese of Killala with rallies in Belmullet and Ballina. Four thousand people from the Deanery of Erris welcomed the Rosary Priest and Dr O'Boyle, the Bishop of Killala, in Belmullet on Wednesday, 2 June 1954. On their arrival at the Barrack Street entrance to the town they were escorted to the square by a guard of honour, formed by local business men. Houses, shops and cottages in Belmullet were newly-painted and the streets were bedecked with flags and bunting. The school children, dressed in white and blue, came to the square in procession from the local school.

In Ballina, Co. Mayo, the closest town to his native parish of Attymass, fifteen thousand assembled in the James Stephens Park, on Sunday, 6 June to listen to the world famous, crusading priest. The dark clouds, which threatened rain all morning, rolled away and the sun shone brightly on the final Rosary Rally in the west. Father Peyton was accompanied by Dr O'Boyle, Bishop of Killala and local clergy, as he entered the park. Father Peyton's voice vibrated with emotion and pride as he spoke of the faith he had inherited from his parents, of his healing and of the crucial importance of family prayer. He appreciated especially the presence that day of 'the people of my own townland and neighbourhood and to see how they accepted and endorsed my poor words.'[8]

Leaving the west behind, Fr Peyton then went north to conduct rallies in Ballymena, Downpatrick and Belfast. Fifteen thousand people from north and mid-Antrim attended the Rosary Rally in Ballymena, Co. Antrim on Thursday, 17 June 1954. A full programme was carried out despite persistent drizzle. Doctor Mageean, Bishop of Down and Connor, who presided, said the rain had made the rally an act of penance, while Fr Peyton spoke in praise of the people who stood patiently in the rain during the ceremony and in doing so gave glory to God. Later the skies cleared, and all was well.

Over one hundred thousand attended the Rosary Crusade rally in the grounds of Our Lady's Hospice,

Beechmount, Belfast. It was the greatest gathering of Belfast Catholics ever, and the biggest crowd to attend any of Fr Peyton's rallies in Ireland.

Eighty thousand assembled in the grounds, and in the nearby Macrory Park there were several thousand mothers with their young children, to whom the ceremonies were relayed. A further one thousand elderly and infirm people were likewise accommodated in the Broadview Cinema and they were afterwards visited by Fr Peyton.

On Sunday, 20 June thirty thousand people gathered in a thirty-acre field outside Downpatrick, Co. Down, for the final rally in the Diocese of Down and Connor. The venue was within sight of the grave of St Patrick, and a few miles from Saul, where the 'Apostle of Ireland' first landed in Ireland. The people listened with rapt attention to Fr Peyton's address and then, led by the children of Downpatrick convent school, they recited fifteen decades of the Rosary. From Ulster the Crusade then moved south into Leinster, to Navan in Co. Meath and Mullingar in Co. Westmeath.

Despite heavy rain, fifteen thousand people from various parts of the Diocese of Meath gathered in Navan on the evening of Thursday, 24 June 1954, to hear Fr Peyton preach on the Family Rosary. They walked in procession from St Mary's Church to the rally in Páirc Tailteann, the local GAA pitch.

The rally in Mullingar was held in Cusack Park. An estimated crowd of seventeen thousand people assembled there, within sight of the twin towers of the cathedral, to listen to Fr Peyton, who spoke with great emotion. Doctor

Kyne, Bishop of Meath, formally welcomed the Rosary Priest to his diocese.

The Diocese of Waterford and Lismore accorded a tumultuous welcome to Fr Peyton at a rally in Dungarvan, in the local show grounds, on Sunday, 11 July. A crowd of almost twenty-five thousand attended the rally, the first of three Rosary rallies arranged by the local bishop, Dr Cohalan.

The second rally in the diocese, which was held in the grounds of St John's College, Waterford City, drew a crowd of forty thousand people on the evening of Wednesday, 14 July. The rally, which embraced the city and a large portion of the county, also attracted thousands of people from other parts of Munster and from Leinster.

The third and final rally in the Diocese of Waterford and Lismore took place on Sunday, 18 July in Clonmel, Co. Tipperary. Despite a clash with the Munster hurling final, involving teams from Cork and Tipperary, over twenty thousand people filled the sportsfield to hear Fr Peyton's stirring address.

The twenty-first and final rally of the Irish Crusade took place on 15 August, the feast of the Assumption, at Our Lady's Island, fourteen miles from Wexford town, in the Diocese of Ferns. Over forty thousand pilgrims were present for the most impressive of all the Irish rallies, 'the greatest religious spectacle ever seen in Co. Wexford.'[9] With so many of the rallies being rain-soaked affairs, it was fitting that the final one was held in glorious sunshine!

Over all, Fr Peyton was very pleased with the outcome of his mission in Ireland. He declared in his autobiography: 'The Irish Crusades were wonderful! Everywhere there was a welcome and a warmness.'[10] His very presence and his words had made an indelible impression on the people, everywhere he went. A west of Ireland reporter commented:

> In my more than twenty years in Irish journalism … never had I come face to face with a man so humble, so saintly, so sincere, so unostentatious, so absorbed in his noble ideal and single-hearted purpose, and so preeminently equipped with the qualities of mind and heart for his glorious global mission as Fr Peyton.[11]

The great crusader priest, however, must have been deeply disappointed that he had not been invited to visit the historic Archdioceses of Armagh, Cashel, and Dublin.

Peyton's energy seemed boundless as he kept up an amazing schedule of rallies and personal appearances, but Fr Ed Murray and other Holy Cross religious worried about his health: 'The rallies take a good deal out of the poor man and he has been completely exhausted during the past few days. It takes episcopal orders to get him to rest. He is so gentle and helpless that he insists upon seeing everyone who wants to see him, the humbler the suppliant the more insistent he is to see the person.'[12]

While it is true that Peyton did seek out and was associated with many rich and famous people in Hollywood and elsewhere, it was always with a view to the promotion of family prayer. Their endorsement of his campaigns won popular support for the cause. The celebrities, in turn, were drawn to him and were happy to play a part his great campaigns. But he always had time too for the ordinary man or woman and for the poor. He never refused a request to pray for another person, whether it be over the phone or when someone asked for some of his time. People with varied problems often called and asked Peyton to pray with them. His favourite response was the *Memorare*. On the street, he often stopped, shook hands with people, and always had something pleasant to say. People's status was of no consequence to him; he treated all people the same.[13]

One morning, while on vacation with his brother Michael in his native Carracastle, a woman from the Travelling Community called to see Fr Peyton who was still asleep in bed. Knowing how much he needed rest, his relatives were loathe to disturb him and told the woman to come back later. She, however, stood her ground and demanded to meet him right away. Meanwhile Fr Peyton, having been awakened by the commotion outside, dressed himself and went out to meet his visitor, whom he greeted warmly. He put her at her ease, saying that he too was a traveller like herself, roaming from place to place and living out of a suitcase. They talked for a while and he gave her his blessing.

© Holy Cross Family Ministries (HCFM)

Devoted parents: Mary and John Peyton instilled in their children a devotion to the holy Rosary and a steadfast belief in the power of prayer.

© HCFM

A family in Christ: Family portrait including John Peyton (front row, second from left); Mary Peyton (front row, second from right); and Patrick's sister Nellie (back row, second from right) with her hand on Patrick's shoulder.

© HCFM

Ordination day: 'The day I gave my heart and soul in love to Mary' is how Fr Peyton (back row, second from right) described his ordination; here he is pictured alongside brother and fellow ordainee Thomas (front row, second from left) at Sacred Heart Church, University of Notre Dame, 15 June 1941.

© HCFM

Capacity crowd: Following an inaugural prayer rally in Ontario, Canada in 1948, Fr Peyton went on to lead more than two hundred and sixty rallies worldwide, including an event in Rio de Janeiro in 1962 (pictured), which attracted a staggering 1.5 million attendees.

© HCFM

A 'living Rosary': an aerial shot of a spectacular display, featuring some three thousand school children, which formed the centrepiece of the Rosary rally that Fr Peyton took to the Melbourne Cricket Ground in November 1951. A choir of twelve thousand children sang the Fatima hymn at the event which included Benediction and a eucharistic procession.

© HCFM

A man of the people: Fr Peyton sharing the Good News with a child in Africa in 1955. During that early African tour, Fr Peyton travelled to Tanzania, Uganda, Kenya and South Africa to promote the faith.

© Bettmann/Getty

'Tea, Father?': Singer Bing Crosby, an early champion of Family Theater of the Air, takes time out on set to prepare a brew for friend and spiritual guide, Fr Peyton, 1956.

© HCFM

Hollywood hero: Father Peyton with a billboard erected near the headquarters of Family Theater Productions, Hollywood, 1984. The slogan 'the family that prays together stays together' inspired Catholics across the globe throughout the twentieth century.

The Hollywood connection 1: Clockwise from left, a then unknown James Dean making his big screen debut as the disciple John in Fr Peyton's Calvary film, *Hill Number One*; Ruth Hussey as the Virgin Mary in the same film; Bobby Driscoll, Rita Johnson and Fr Peyton sharing the gift of the Rosary with listeners of Mutual Broadcasting System.

© HCFM

The Hollywood connection 2: Above, showbiz heavyweights Jimmy Stewart, Don Ameche and Loretta Young bring their talents to bear on Fr Peyton's Family Theater of the Air; below, Fr Peyton flanked by comedians Jack Benny and Lucille Ball.

© HCFM

© HCFM

An inspiration: Fr Peyton, with Rosary beads in hand,
greeting Pope John Paul II in 1987 (above)
and, in contemplative mode, praying with Mother Teresa (below) in 1981.
Fr Peyton's indefatigable commitment to promoting prayer won the
admiration of Christian leaders around the world.

© HCFM

CHAPTER 7

ASIAN AND AFRICAN CAMPAIGNS

Following his mission in Ireland, Peyton resumed his international crusades with a return to Spain, to the Dioceses of Vitoria, San Sebastián, Bilbao, Tarragona and Santander. The two main rallies proved to be very successful, each one attracting around one hundred and twenty thousand people.

Perhaps his busiest and most demanding schedule ever was the period from mid-November 1954 until September 1955. This major campaign began with a four-month crusade in fifty-nine archdioceses and dioceses of the nations of India, Pakistan, Burma, Sri Lanka, Malaysia and Thailand. Peyton addressed thirty-seven rallies – the largest being in Mumbai (Bombay) in India and Colombo, in Sri Lanka – where crowds of two hundred thousand and one hundred thousand respectively heard him speak.

Father Quinn was delighted with the success of the crusade in Asia and wrote to his superior general:

> It (the crusade) made a tremendous impression on all, Catholics and non-Catholics alike. The Buddhist papers have been enthusiastic in spreading the message and taking as their slogan that: 'The family

that prays together stays together' and one of them reminds us that 'it is indeed welcoming in these days of materialism and strife that there is still so much faith and hope in spiritual values.'[1]

From Asia, the Crusade moved to the continent of Africa, where he was to labour for seven months. He began with the South African campaign, which covered thirty-one archdioceses and dioceses. Eight rallies were conducted, with the highest attendance of twenty-eight thousand at Johannesburg. Father Tom Gill, a local pastor, was generous in his praise of Fr Peyton when he wrote to James Connerton CSC:

> There can be no possible doubt that Fr Peyton was a phenomenal personal success here during his African Family Rosary Crusade. There can be no doubt either about the burning sincerity, the tireless energy, the simple but convincing eloquence, the quite indescribable hold that he had over the extraordinarily diverse audience here.[2]

Gill continued: 'He has endeared himself to one and all, and he has taught us that the Rosary is laden with love and peace and security, and we thank God that he made it possible for the Ambassador of His Beloved Mother to visit Africa.'[3]

The South African campaign was followed immediately by one in East Africa, by far the largest such campaign to date. It consisted of seventy-four archdioceses and dioceses in six East African countries: Kenya, Tanganyika (Tanzania),

Rhodesia (Zimbabwe), Nyasaland (Malawi), Uganda, and the Sudan.

During their time in Kenya an incident occurred which put Fr Peyton's faith in Mary's protection to the test. As the team was returning to base one evening, on their guard's advice they took a short detour through a huge game preserve, to view the wild animals in their natural habitat. Father Joseph Quinn, CSC, takes up the story:

> As we entered the jungle area in our small Volkswagen we spotted a group of ten or fifteen giraffes grazing on the hillside. Father Peyton suggested we stop our car and take a closer look. While we were watching, four or five lions joined the giraffe and a herd of wildebeests came across the hill. In the distance, we could see a hyena darting towards a small cluster of gazelle. Since this was our first encounter with the wild animals that we had read about and heard about since childhood, Fr Peyton and I especially were jumping with wonderment at the scene before our eyes.
>
> As the sun began to set, we got back in the car and Fr Collerton turned the key. Nothing happened. He turned it several more times and still the motor refused to turn over. We opened up the hood and since all of us were non-professional mechanics, the best we could do was tap a few parts with a screwdriver and kick the tyres to see if they were full of air and then to honk the horn to make sure that the battery wasn't dead. After all these attempts failed, Fr Peyton suggested that we get back in the

car and say the Joyful Mysteries of the Rosary, asking Our Blessed Mother to help get the motor started.

After the Joyful Mysteries, Father Ned and I again got out and looked at the motor. We found an old crank in the back seat and each of us took turns cranking the car to no avail. Again, Fr Peyton called us into the car to say the Sorrowful Mysteries of the Rosary. Instead of meditating on the Mysteries of the Rosary, since it was getting very dark, my mind was imagining an elephant drifting over our way and gently tipping our Volkswagen over or, I could hear in the distance, the lions growling before dashing off for their supper! I knew I was supposed to be prepared for death, but it did not seem like this was the type of death I wanted to suffer. When we finished saying the Sorrowful Mysteries, Fr Ned and I took turns on the crank again and on my final turn, before my arm was about to fall out if its socket, the motor turned over and we were able to get the car going.

By now it was pitch dark and with nothing but the stars and the fearsome noises of the wild beasts we started back towards Nairobi. After a few moments of driving Fr Peyton relieved us all by asking us to join with him in saying the Glorious Mysteries of the Rosary in thanksgiving for our escape from the jungle that night.[4]

In addition to speaking at all thirty-two rallies, Fr Peyton also visited Catholic institutions, especially hospitals, giving support to thousands who were sick, crippled or handicapped. The challenging climate, however, took a toll on Peyton in the form of severe heatstroke. Nevertheless, his crusade in Africa was very successful and widely acclaimed:

> Father Peyton certainly gained overwhelming victories for Our Blessed Lady in South, East and Central Africa. From every territory, glowing reports have come from archbishops, bishops, priests and religious testifying to the phenomenal success of the crusade and its lasting results.[5]

The Crusade returned to Spain, in February 1956, beginning in Santiago de Compostela. In the following year Peyton took the Crusade to the Dioceses of Salamanca, Badajoz and Albacete, where he encountered for the first time the Spanish Misionaras – female members of a Spanish secular institute, Instituto Misioneras Seculares – who lived in community, much like religious, but wore no habit. The Misioneras engaged in a wide range of professional and secretarial activities, always on behalf on an apostolic activity and with the approval of the bishop of the diocese in which the work was conducted. In 1956 Fr Peyton sought the Misionaras' help with the Crusades in Spain and internationally.

One such helper was Margarita de Lecea. When she was only twelve years old in her native Bilbao, Margarita read one day about a priest in Hollywood who was persuading film stars to help him promote family prayer, and she was so delighted that she wrote him a letter of encouragement and congratulation. Little did she then think that she would, years later, be assigned by her superiors to work with him in the same apostolate. She worked with the Family Rosary Crusade in Spain, in the Philippines and in Latin America. The help of the Misionaras in Spain was very much appreciated by the Crusade team, but their assistance was critical in the Latin American crusades in the 1960s.

CHAPTER 8

CRUSADE UNDER SCRUTINY

In preparation for the Latin American Crusades, Fr Peyton commissioned the production of fifteen half-hour films on the Mysteries of the Rosary, which were produced in Spain in 1956, using top-level producers, scriptwriters and musicians. The films, which were in Eastmancolor for projection on a panoramic screen, were financed largely by donations from convents in the USA, Ireland and elsewhere. Father Peyton decided that the films should be shown for the first time to an international audience at the 1958 Brussels World Fair, in a specially constructed three-hundred seat cinema under the Vatican Pavilion. Daily screenings, from noon to 8 p.m. continuously, were held in English, Spanish, Walloon and French. A survey showed that viewers responded most positively to the sorrowful mysteries, with the glorious and joyful next in ranked significance. Over five months, two hundred and fifty thousand people saw two or more films.

Among those who viewed the films was Auxiliary Bishop Leo Josef (later Cardinal) Suenens of Brussels. He was then relatively unknown outside his own country but was destined to acquire fame for his theological and pastoral leadership at the Second Vatican Council. He was enthusiastic about what he saw, with the film on the Assumption making the deepest impression on him. He wanted to arrange a Crusade in Brussels right away, but his archbishop was unwilling to underwrite the substantial cost. Bishop Suenens did, however, introduce Peyton to Bishop Émile-Josef de Smedt of Bruges who requested a Crusade in his diocese of one million Catholics. The Crusade, which was held during April, May and June 1959, proved to be an overwhelming success in what was a sophisticated and highly industrialised area.

Key to its success was Sr Marie Eymard, a Belgian nun, who acted as interpreter at the preparatory meetings and at the rallies. In addition, she prepared manuals for religious instruction in the schools, based on the fifteen Rosary films, which were being used for the first time. Four rallies were held with sixty-five thousand in attendance at Kortrijk.

Afterwards, Bishop de Smedt undertook a serious analysis of the impact the Crusade had on the diocese. He issued his report on the Crusade in the form of a five-thousand-word letter to his priests. First, he thanked and congratulated the clergy, nearly all of whom had put into action the campaign plan presented by the Crusade team. Most parishes had no difficulty in finding the laymen needed to visit each ten families. Thirty-five thousand men had been recruited as visitors and eight hundred thousand had pledged to join each day in family prayer. At the beginning many thought there was no prospect of success because of the influence of materialism, which had caused family prayer to disappear, but the facts had contradicted those considerations.

The diocese had experienced, in the bishop's words, 'an extraordinary intervention of divine grace. It is evident that the Holy Spirit, by the intercession of the Mother of God, has poured upon the members of Christ's Mystical Body special graces of light and strength.'[1] The prayers of the people for the success of the Crusade had borne fruit and the Holy Spirit had crushed 'with a sledgehammer blow' the belief that it is impossible to find men willing to cooperate in a purely religious apostolate. Again, public opinion had been mobilised by newspapers, radio and television and by the preaching in all churches on five consecutive Sundays. Father Peyton had made such good use of all the media that, the bishop said, '… at the end of the Crusade there was not a single family in the diocese which was not aware of what was going on.'[2]

Bishop Smedt then made some pertinent remarks on the way Fr Peyton conducted the rally:

> It is not without reason that Fr Peyton attaches so much importance to the rallies. He seeks to put into action the psychology of the masses for the benefit of the cause he defends. Everyone has been able to see clearly that there was no question of excitement or demagogy.
>
> Father Peyton was keen to ensure a very serene and deep religious atmosphere at each and every rally. It was touching to see how very humbly he put the influence radiating from his person in the service of Jesus and Mary, never giving the least importance to his own person.[3]

Bishop de Smedt then addressed the matter of the depth and permanence of the Crusade's impact on the diocese. He declared, referring to the Crusade, 'The hour of grace has struck'.[4]

It was now over to the parochial clergy to profit from this moment and 'to build up systematically the apostolate of the neighbourhood.'[5] Father Peyton found the bishop's report to be very helpful in evaluating the strengths and weaknesses of the Crusade, which had begun in London, Ontario in 1947 and to which he pragmatically added one feature after another.

Father Peyton had a longstanding invitation to take the crusade to the Philippines, which he finally accepted late in 1959. The Crusade took place between 1 November and 10 December. Four rallies were held, with one million in attendance in Cebu and 1.5 million at Luneta Park, Manila, despite the torrential tropical rains that preceded Fr Peyton's address. The Rosary priest was overjoyed at his reception: 'Never in all the history of the Crusades have I come to an area or country that is responding like the Philippines. No one is holding back.'[6] Joseph Quinn CSC commented: 'The Crusade in Manila was without doubt the greatest we have had in any part of the world.'[7]

The success of the crusade led to the establishment of the first permanent international Family Rosary office and the appointment of a director.

CHAPTER 9

LATIN-AMERICAN CRUSADES 1959–66

The Family Rosary Crusade had been experienced in every continent by the late 1950s, except in South America. Peyton looked forward very much to visiting there to rekindle and deepen the faith of the people. While 95 per cent of the people were baptised, only one third of that number had received their first Communion. Only 6 per cent of men and 12 per cent of women attended Mass. Priests were very scarce and the official Church tended to side, unduly, with the property owners and the wealthy. There was also the looming threat of Communism, which was already gaining a foothold in Cuba.

Chile was selected as the first country in Latin America to host a Rosary Crusade. Peyton planned three crusades, encompassing the entire nation along its more than two thousand seven-hundred-mile length. For the purposes of the national Crusade the country was divided in three: Santiago and the middle third first, followed by the northern region and finally, the south. Here the Crusade proper was preceded by the Popular Mission, the showing of the Rosary films followed by a carefully prepared catechesis. Just as the early Franciscan and Dominican missionaries used picture books to teach the native people about Jesus' life, death and Resurrection, so Peyton and his team brought with them to Latin America the Rosary films to evangelise and educate the people in the basic teachings of the faith. The Popular Mission, which was very effective, became a feature of all the crusades in Latin America. Father Peyton described the process as 'evangelisation for the masses'. The transportation of the seventeen tonnes of equipment needed for the Popular Mission, including projectors, transformers, mobile generators and cans of film, was indeed an onerous task.

In Santiago, and the middle third of Chile, the Popular Mission proved to be a great success. The local bishop then issued a pastoral letter introducing five weeks of parish homilies and meetings with parishes, schools, and other institutions. The Crusade concluded with rallies and the pledge drives. Over half a million people took part in the largest rally in the capital, Santiago. In the northern region five rallies were held between 26 June and 24 July 1960. Father Quinn CSC reported to his superiors that the Crusade had been a great success in the centre and northern parts of Chile. In the south, which had been devastated by a recent earthquake, the rallies were sparsely attended.

Pope Pius XII, in a letter to Fr Peyton dated 4 April 1958, shortly before he died, praised the newly commissioned Rosary films, which he had viewed. He described the fifteen films as 'a massive undertaking that has been achieved with distinction.' He continued:

> These films have an apostolic character and value, quite beyond their technical and artistic perfection ... They open up the book of God's revelation to

man; they turn the pages of a divine love story for those to read who will and reading to understand the infinite yearning of God for the creature of his omnipotence. Nazareth, Bethlehem, the towns of the Jordan valley, and dear unhappy Jerusalem, all play their part in portraying the successive phases of the redemptive work of the Incarnate Son of God. As the scenes of that life pass before the eyes, contemplation becomes more fervent, love grows more ardently, allegiance is firmer ... Blessed will be the faithful who have the good fortune, let us say the precious grace, to see these films. We sincerely hope their number will be legion.[1]

The successor of Pius XII, Pope John XXIII, also endorsed Peyton's unique ministry in South America in a letter on 1 May 1959:

We have been informed that you are beginning a new stage in the apostolate which has characteristically distinguished your life. With the technical help of motion pictures to show the meaning, value and excellence of the Mysteries of the Rosary, you wish to increase devotion to the Holy Rosary in Latin America.[2]

The pontiff reminded Fr Peyton that Christopher Columbus' flagship was called the 'Sancta Maria'; Mary, 'the same name which missionaries were to spread on the mountain tops, in the plains and in the jungles.'[3] Pope John XXIII also referred to the graces and blessings which family prayer can bring to homes:

> When parents and children gather together at the
> end of the day in the recitation of the Rosary,
> together they meditate on the example of work,
> obedience and charity which shone in the house of
> Nazareth; together they learn from the Mother of
> God to suffer serenely; to accept with dignity and
> courage the difficulties of life and to acquire the
> proper attitude to the daily events of life. It is certain
> that they will meet with greater facility the problems
> of family life. Homes will, thereby, be converted
> into sanctuaries of peace.[4]

Peter Grace, who had been deeply moved on seeing the
Rosary films at the Brussels World Fair in 1958, agreed
to finance five hundred thousand dollars to bring the films
to the poor and illiterate in South America. With Grace's
support Peyton was confident that the Popular Mission in
Latin America would be adequately financed.

The crusades held in the big cities of Latin America
required a great deal of planning. The first step was the
formation of a team of specialists who very quickly
became known as 'Our Lady's gypsies', because they lived
out of suitcases, constantly flitting from place to place.
The basic team consisted of two priests backed up by five
of the Misionaras who were doubly useful because
Spanish was their mother tongue. The high level of their
education, combined with the similarity of the Spanish
and Portuguese languages, enabled them to work in Brazil
almost as efficiently as in Spanish speaking countries.

A Crusade was planned in phases: The Popular
Mission; the hospitals, armed forces, prisons; school

campaign, the universities, parish campaign, publicity and public relations activities – all of them culminating in the rally and the collection of pledges. Two local priests were assigned full time by the bishop to participate in all the planning, one as diocesan director for the Crusade, and the other as director of the Popular Mission. They knew the priests and the people, the local customs and prejudices.

The Popular Mission was designed to ensure that every Catholic in the city, but particularly the illiterate and the poor, would get a basic course in Christian doctrine in a way that they were capable of understanding, namely, by the projection of the fifteen Rosary films. Through them they were shown the life of Christ in a context that stressed its relevance to the problems they encountered in their lives and in their own families.

To achieve the desired saturation coverage, the Crusade team began with an intensive reconnaissance of the entire city, plotting on a large map the individual parishes and the sites in each parish most suitable for outdoor projection of the films at night, such as public squares or athletic fields not identified with a parish church. In most Latin American cities, the climate lends itself to outdoor viewing. Since most of the people didn't have the money to go to the cinema, the free show was a novelty that quickly generated its own publicity.

The parish priest chose four local men for each projector site, two to operate the film projector and two to give commentary and instruction at the end of each film. Courses lasting about two weeks were organised by the Misioneras. Women volunteers, who would go door-to-door inviting people to attend the films, were given four training sessions. Two weeks before the first film was shown the region was flooded with advertising, including handbills distributed by the volunteers, billboards, and cars with loudspeakers, as well as the use of radio and television.

Two films were shown per night, for a week, making a programme that ran for a little more than an hour, depending on the length of the commentaries. Only one film remained to be viewed on the last night, but the programme was completed by a Mass, preceded by confessions. At that point, the impact of the Popular Mission became evident, with large numbers of people joining long queues for confession.

The programme for the sick in the hospitals, for prisoners, and for the armed forces followed the same procedure. Instructors and operators were chosen from among those who worked in the parishes. It was noted that many of the men who offered themselves for the additional work had never done any work for the Church. The sick and those in jail were asked to offer their hardships for the success of the Crusade and for the renewal of family life in their country. Almost all of them gladly went on record by signing a pledge to that effect.

Peyton was seen by many as someone who could help with the fight against Communism. A radio broadcast editorial commented:

> With Khrushchev and Communism threatening to destroy the world, the work of Fr Patrick J. Peyton becomes of greater importance to every individual

living today. And when Communism is overcome ... as it will be ... one of the great factors in the triumph of religion and freedom and decency will be the work of this humble priest who is convincing mankind that ... the world that prays together stays together.[5]

When commissioning the Rosary films in Spain, Peyton had in mind that they would be used exclusively to educate people about Christ and spread Marian devotion and family prayer. He was pleased, however, when people told him that the films were also helping to roll back the advance of Communism in Latin America. Peyton had the films quickly dubbed into Spanish and Portuguese, declaring, 'We are determined to wage a prayer and catechetical offensive – a real positive answer to the Communist exploitation of our brothers and sisters in South America.'[6]

The next move was to Caracas in Venezuela, a city where, Peyton believed, Communist influence was growing: 'Caracas was chosen for a Crusade because it was another Havana, ready for revolution, very restless and disturbed.'[7]

The Popular Mission was interrupted on a few occasions by Communist sympathisers, including stone throwers who inflicted some minor damage to equipment. The crusade included the extensive use of Family Theater television films, produced in the 1950s. Despite the efforts by Communists to disrupt the event, including a bomb threat, the rally held in Caracas on 16 July 1961 attracted five hundred and fifty thousand people.

Peter Grace was especially pleased with Peyton's ability to break through Communist opposition. In a letter to his provincial and superior he declared:

> Father Peyton has demonstrated that he can saturate an area in a few months in a manner which is devastating to the Communist cause merely by turning the attention of the people to their God and their faith, which Communism must, of course, destroy in order to win victory.[8]

In the summer of 1962 the Crusade came to Recife in the state of Pernambuco in northern Brazil. Father Christopher O'Toole CSC was very pleased that Peyton had finally come to the largest country in Latin America, where his Crusade was urgently needed:

> I am so happy that you are now working in Brazil. God knows now is the time to exert all the influence possible to counteract the evils of Communism in that country. At last the hierarchy and the clergy of Latin America are becoming aware of the fact that it is not Protestantism they have to worry about, but Communism.[9]

The Crusade in Recife proceeded without complications and was well received by the local people and greatly appreciated by Church officials. The main rally of five hundred thousand people was a great success. A local newspaper called the Crusade the 'greatest triumph of any Catholic movement in our cities for decades' and declared that 'the success of the Recife Crusade pushed back tremendously the Communist forces.'[10] The visit inspired Peyton to produce a twenty-five-minute documentary, *Smile of Recife,* for use in future Popular Missions.

The Rio de Janeiro campaign was the largest undertaking of the Family Rosary Crusade to date. The huge area involved presented many challenges. The city was divided into four sectors with two separate crusade offices. To serve the large population, the films were shown on local television (as well as in parishes, schools, hospitals and other institutions) on fifteen consecutive evenings. On 8 December, the Feast of the Immaculate Conception, the people of Rio witnessed the marvellous spectacle of an illuminated Rosary thirty metres in length, with a cross eight metres tall, adorning the famous Christ the Redeemer statue, which overlooks the city.

The rally in Rio, which took place on 16 December, was attended by 1.5 million people, the biggest crowd in the history of the Rosary Crusade. Father George DePrizio CSC has left us a vivid description of that memorable day:

> Almost two hours before the scheduled event and already a great crowd had gathered. Perhaps a hundred thousand were waiting. Father Peyton went immediately into the nearby church to pray. About three thirty, a half hour or so before the rally time, I went to report to him.
>
> 'There must be at least half a million people.'
>
> 'Thank God,' he whispered between Hail Mary's.
>
> 'That's good. Brazilians come late. We'll have a million, I'm sure, when the time comes.'

And a million he did have – for by four o'clock the crowd was immense. When I mounted the high platform erected on the main avenue of the city and looked out into the crowd, I felt that only on judgement day would I once again witness such a vast assembly. People – people – people. As far as the human eye could see. It seemed that all of Rio was there. A short distance away the famous Copacabana beach was almost deserted. And the huge city, that a short time before was tingling with its bosa nova and doing its samba, quieted down and turned to Mary ... turned to prayer as five representative families led the multitude in the five Glorious Mysteries of the Rosary ... and turned to listen to Mary's apostle as he electrified the crowd.

For forty minutes Fr Pat pleaded Mary's cause for Family Prayer. I shall never forget the image of this man of God and Mary holding a million and more people with his strong, simple words. There were moments when it seemed his very heart would break and all his love and affection and tenderness for Our Lady would spill out and engulf that crowd. There were moments, too, when he seemed like a great prophet, not a prophet of doom, but a prophet promising peace, and blessing through Mary and family prayer.

All of a sudden it was over. The cardinal rose to express his gratitude and the crowd sang a hymn to Our Lady, and the national anthem was sung as it had never been sung before ... When Fr Peyton descended from the high stage it was necessary to call the police to protect him. Thousands surged forward trying to touch his cassock, pleading for his blessing and prayer.

Minutes later Fr Peyton was in the church again before the high altar. I went to congratulate him. He said, 'Tell the priests and missionaries to come at once for a holy hour of thanksgiving.'

And there in all the sweat and exhaustion of his massive frame he poured out his thanks to God and Mary. For the next three days the entire staff of priests and secular missionaries gathered with Fr Pat for a holy hour at a church dedicated to Our Lady of Glory.[11]

Besides Church officials, the event was attended by President Goulart. Dom Hélder Câmara, auxiliary bishop of the city, expressed the hope of many in commenting after the rally, 'God willing, the Family Rosary Crusade will never leave Brazil. It is a movement that finds a deep echo in the Brazilian soul.'[12]

The Crusade's next destination was Salvador in the state of Bahia, in the north east of Brazil. It was conducted there from 8 April to 6 June 1963. The Crusade experienced more hostility there than in any other part of Brazil. There seemed to be a hostility against all things 'American'. The rally, which was held on 2 June, was attended by the Brazilian primate, Cardinal Don Augusto Álvaro da Silva, the state governor and the mayor of Salvador. The gathering ended with the six hundred thousand faithful waving a 'sea of handkerchiefs', as an expression of popular affection for Peyton.[13]

The Crusade in Salvador was conducted almost simultaneously with one in Belo Horizonte, the capital of the state of Minas Gerais, located in the east-central zone of the nation. The team arrived on 28 February 1963 and set up an office in mid-March. The films were shown in three parish sectors, then in schools, hospitals, prisons and military barracks with 2.1 million in attendance. As in Rio, the films were also shown on local television. The rally was held on 16 June and drew some five hundred thousand people.

The Crusade team took a well-earned break before moving to Porto Alegre, the capital city of the state of Rio Grande do Sul, in southern Brazil. The Popular Mission, though marred by inclement weather, did arouse the interest of residents to the films and their message. A local journalist commented, 'This effort of Fr Peyton can be called, from a motion picture standpoint, the most fantastic Motion Picture Club in the history of humanity.'[14] One member of the local hierarchy was pleased with the Crusade's ability to transform people and spur their faith: 'I think that the movement has a wonderful motive and an enrichment of doctrine, and it is carried out in an active way. I am certain that the Crusade here will also bring many people to God, through the hands of Our Lady.'[15]

The Family Day celebration was introduced on the Feast of the Immaculate Conception, 8 December 1963. In Brazil the commemoration was led by President Goulart, who declared 8 December as Family Day throughout the whole country. Joseph Quinn CSC put together an hour-long television special that originated from Rio de Janeiro but was broadcast throughout South

America. Among the many celebrities taking part were Pele, and Bing Crosby who sang 'Ave Maria'.

The Crusade's next and greatest challenge was the Archdiocese of São Paulo, the largest city in Brazil and the largest archdiocese in the world, with a population of approximately six million people. The recruitment and training of enough laymen and laywomen for the Popular Mission and other Crusade functions alone, was a mammoth task. In addition, the political and religious situation was highly unstable.

Quinn warned Peyton that many groups wanted to use the Crusade to advance their own agenda. Peyton had to keep the Crusade independent of any group or political position: 'One of the greatest problems here in São Paulo is the political situation at this moment. There are attempts to use the Rosary to further the political aims of some groups.'[16]

The superior general, Christopher O'Toole CSC said: 'I think the danger we must avoid is that of permitting any political party to identify itself with us.'[17] Matters took a turn for the worse with the resignation of Cardinal Carlos Motta of São Paulo followed by the overthrow of the government by a military coup, led by the army chief of staff, Castelo Branco. The coup was over by 1 April and Branco, who was proclaimed president, was inaugurated on 15 April.

Peyton and his team were not deterred by these events but proceeded with the opening of the Popular Mission on 6 April. An estimated 4.3 million viewed the films, shown on eighty projector sets in seven parish sectors and employing seven hundred projectionists and four hundred and seventy catechists. The rally, which was described by

Peyton as an 'extraordinary triumph' was held on 16 August and drew two million visitors, the largest crowd ever to attend such an event in the history of the Family Rosary Crusade.

The role of the Family Rosary Crusade in the political revolution in Brazil was much debated afterwards. Dom Hélder Câmara, auxiliary bishop of Rio, attributed the fall of Goulart's government, which was about to legalise the Communist Party, to the work of the Crusade. The new president paid tribute to the Crusade, saying how much he admired it. The great rally in Rio de Janeiro had helped to form the public opinion of the Brazilian people and gave them the courage to bring about the revolution of 31 March.

The Holy Cross community was in no doubt that the Crusade had been a catalyst in precipitating the revolution. Father Peyton certainly believed so:

> As you are aware … much credit is given by great leaders in the Church and State in Brazil to the Family Rosary Crusade in the overthrow of the Goulart government that was moving the country rapidly into communistic control. Overnight the situation was changed without a drop of blood. The credit is being given by great leaders … to Our Blessed Mother and the Family Rosary Crusade for having done this.[18]

Richard Sullivan CSC, who assumed the reins of the Eastern Province in April 1964 and attended the São Paulo rally, wrote to the superior general:

More than once I heard it said that the success of the revolution which saved Brazil from Communism was due in great part to Father Peyton and the Rosary. One secular paper editorial stated that in history this revolution would take its place alongside Lepanto's victory through the Rosary.[19]

This is a reference to the famous naval battle of 1571 when Christian forces defeated the Ottoman Turks at Lepanto, through, it was believed, the intercession of Our Lady of the Rosary. Cardinal Carlo Confalonierei, President of the Pontifical Commission for Latin America, wrote to Peyton, 'The pontifical Commission greatly appreciates your work among the Latin American peoples and considers your mass apostolate to be an effective contribution to the progress of the Catholic life in these countries.'[20]

Many sources continued to applaud the Crusade for turning the tide of religious faith, tilting the balance of power away from Communism and toward greater co-operation and social justice and creating a 'powerful lay apostolate': 'In South America, in the short space of five years, the Crusade had shown itself a most powerful means of catechising masses of people, whom the conventional structures of the Church do not reach because of the shortage of priests.'[21]

Independent observers of the Crusade were also vocal in their praise. A São Paulo journalist wrote, 'I observed, from the commencement of the Family Rosary Crusade in Recife until now, the great influence which it has on the conscience of Brazilians. Before the revolution, one slept with pistols in our beds but now, thanks to the influence of the Crusade, we can sleep in peace.'[22]

Another writer commented, 'And the Rosary brought about the miracle of the cohesion of all forces, brought their spirits together, unified their wills, consolidated the ties which existed between the people's aspirations and the patriotic vigilance of the Armed Forces.'[23]

The Congregation of Holy Cross proudly boasted of the merit of Peyton and the Crusade as paragons in response to the call of the Holy Father for action in South America. In 1961 George DePrizio CSC, provincial of the Eastern Province, urged its members to join Peyton and the Crusade, thus answering the Vatican's call for missionary help in Latin America. He extolled Peyton to the general:

> Anyone who says that Fr Peyton's Crusade is merely a superficial and emotional stirring of the people aroused just for the occasion simply does not know what he is talking about. I have never seen such a vital demonstration of faith before in all my life and I am convinced that only God knows the wonderful things that are wrought through it.[24]

Lalande, the superior general, was equally generous when responding to the provincial:

> I thank God for the good he chooses to accomplish through the instrumentality of Fr Peyton. In these decades Fr Peyton is to your province and the congregation as a whole what, in his time, Brother

Andre (St Andre) was to Holy Cross in Canada and to the whole congregation. These are men whose message and influence escape geographical bounds.[25]

Because the US government saw the Family Rosary Crusade as a force for good in Latin America, and realised that it was powerful in combatting the rise of Communism there, it offered financial aid to Peyton to further his campaigns. As a result, Peyton was compelled to share control of the location and timing of Crusade events. He found this arrangement acceptable so long as his Marian mission remained at the forefront. He never lost focus on his priority and continued to foster the Family Rosary as fervently and zealously as before. However, the policy of accepting financial support from the CIA ceased eventually on 30 June 1966, following strong objections from Church authorities.

Peyton's Latin American campaign was next directed towards the Dominican Republic, probably the most religiously illiterate nation that the Crusade had entered. The Church has been repressed for thirty-one years under the dictatorship of Rafael Trujillo. The Popular Mission, which began in mid-February, was marred by rock-throwing and even a couple of Molotov cocktails. Although screenings were disrupted by acts of vandalism, the films were shown to over two million people. Six rallies were held, the largest being in Santo Domingo which drew a crowd of two hundred and fifty thousand people on 21 March 1965. The Crusade then moved to Panama. It was conducted on a national level from 20

June to 1 August 1965, beginning with the Popular Mission. It culminated with a national rally in Panama which attracted two hundred and fifty thousand.

From Panama, the Crusade returned to South America and to Quito in Ecuador. The Crusade there concluded on 27 February 1966, following six rallies, the largest of which was attended by one hundred thousand in Quito. The Crusade then moved to Guayaquil, Ecuador's largest city. Here, once again, the Family Rosary Crusade encountered religious apathy and even indifference, a sign of latent hostility towards the Church, from political forces. The word 'Rosary' seemed to antagonise some to the extent that it was suggested that the title 'Family Rosary' be replaced by 'Family Unity' in advertisements. Nonetheless, the major rally, held in Guayaquil on 14 August 1966 was attended by two hundred and twenty thousand, a figure reported in a local paper as 'unprecedented in the history of Guayaquil'.

The conclusion of the campaign in Ecuador ended the Family Rosary Crusade in Latin America for the immediate future. The Institute of Secular Missionaries, which had played such a significant role in the Latin American Crusades, chose not to continue with Peyton's work. In the spirit of aggiornamento ('bringing up to date') that was characteristic of the Second Vatican Council, the Institute decided that individual members should be free to choose their apostolates, rather than being assigned one. A second blow was the loss of Fr William Belyea CSC, the only qualified Spanish-speaking member of the team, who left the Crusade to study psychology in Canada.

Father Peyton could certainly boast of the efficacy of the Crusades in Latin America. Between September 1959 and October 1965, the Crusades were conducted in forty-two dioceses with a total population of nearly twenty-eight million people. More than twenty-three million attended the films, which were shown by over two thousand six hundred technicians and a similar number of catechists; nine million attended the rallies; and over two hundred radio and television stations aired the Family Rosary commercials, Family Theater shows, and various films. More importantly for Peyton, his message of family prayer through the Rosary had now been proclaimed on every continent.

CHAPTER 10

BRINGING CHRIST
TO THE MASSES

During his Latin American campaign Peyton took occasional breaks to conduct rallies elsewhere. In the autumn of 1961 Peyton was back on US soil conducting a crusade in San Francisco, at the invitation of Archbishop John J. Mitty. The Crusade front team, headed by Joseph Quinn CSC, had arrived there in August to make the necessary preparations. The archbishop duly issued his pastoral letter, urging his people to participate in the campaign. The Popular Mission – the showing of the Rosary Films – did not feature in this Crusade. The crusade culminated on 7 October with a grand rally at the polo field in San Francisco's Golden Gate Park, which drew a crowd of five hundred thousand. Successful smaller rallies were held in Sacramento, Redding and Eureka in the latter half of the month.

Early in 1962 Fr Peyton paid a return visit to the Philippines at the request of the bishops of ten dioceses. The preparations for the crusade were made by Joseph Quinn CSC, Francis Grogan CSC, Bienvenido Lopez, a Filipino priest, and two members of the Irish Auxiliaries, Gertie Lally and Pearl Buckley. Father Peyton was present for the rallies, as was his normal mode of operation. Once again, the crowds at the rallies were phenomenal, with two hundred thousand present in San Fernando on 28 January, two million at Cebu on 4 March, and five hundred thousand in Naga in the Archdiocese of Caceres, on 11 March.

Because of the success of the Philippines Crusade Peyton decided to conduct a post-Crusade Popular Mission in the dioceses he had first visited in 1959. This involved showing the fifteen Rosary Films, preceded by a new film, *The Redeemer*. The Popular Mission commenced in January 1966, starting in Manila and reaching all the dioceses visited in the previous crusade within one year.

Buoyed up by his experience in the Philippines, Peyton was inspired to go next to Spain. The Popular Mission there differed very much from elsewhere. Francis Grogan CSC and Robert Pelton SC suggested to Peyton that he show the films not only to the poor, the target groups in Latin America and the Philippines, but to the wealthy as well. Consequently, the films were shown in the homes of prominent Madrid residents, leading to greater support for the Crusade and even inspiring some to become catechists.

The Popular Mission was conducted in Madrid between May 1963 and June 1964. The region was divided into fifteen sectors, with two films shown per night for eight nights. Peyton firmly believed in the efficacy of this effort, expressing his basic creed of bringing Christ to the masses: 'By means of the films the Crusade has developed an extraordinary force and power to penetrate the hearts and minds of the poor, the religiously uninformed, the masses lost to the Church and her sacraments.'[1]

The Madrid Crusade reached its climax with the rally held on 31 May 1964, which was attended by an estimated one million people. Bernard Mullahy CSC, Assistant Superior General, who witnessed the rally, lauded Peyton and the Family Crusade in a letter to the provincial, Richard Sullivan:

> I never felt prouder of Holy Cross than I did when I witnessed the tremendous work it accomplished in the Archdiocese of Madrid. Holy Cross has indeed been singularly blessed by having had this apostolate confided to it, and your province is especially fortunate to have this extraordinary opportunity to carry on a worldwide apostolate of such intensity and impact.[2]

From Madrid, the Crusade travelled to Barcelona where a rally was held on 28 February 1965, and then on to the Canary Islands for a series of Rosary campaigns. From September 1965 to December 1966 Crusades were conducted in Las Palmas, Santa Cruz de Tenerife, and Palma de Mallorca. The core crusade was assisted by members of the Focolare movement, a lay and clerical group, who carried out the duties which the secular missionaries used to perform.

The twentieth anniversary of the foundation of Family Theater was marked by a one hundred dollar-a-plate banquet in the Beverly Hilton Hotel in Hollywood on 8 September 1962. Over one hundred sponsors were engaged in organising the event, with a fundraising target of one hundred and fifty thousand dollars. Among the one thousand six hundred-people attending were many of the celebrities who took part in Family Theater over the years, including Ann Blyth, Raymond Burr, Loretta Young and Irene Dunne. J. Peter Grace, Luke Hart, Supreme Knight of the Knights of Columbus and former vice president Richard Nixon were also in attendance. Congratulatory telegrams were received from Pope John XXIII, President John F. Kennedy and Edmund Brown, Governor of California. The Superior General of Holy Cross, Germain Lalande, CSC, spoke of Peyton as God's instrument: 'Fr Peyton's vocation cannot be explained by mere human reasoning. It is obviously a mandate from God Himself ... We offer Fr Peyton our homage, our respect, and our prayers for continual success in all that he is doing for God, Our Lady, and family life.'[3]

During the 1960s many personal and ministerial awards were received by Fr Peyton in recognition of his life's work. As had been the case with Pope Pius XII, both John XXIII and Paul VI wrote to him, praising his ministry and congratulating him on his accomplishments. Paul VI made special reference to the Family Rosary Crusade in his remarks:

> We are pleased to note that in the past twenty-one years, the Family Rosary Crusade has carried the message of family prayer to the peoples of thirty-two countries ... We cherish the prayerful hope that the zealous endeavours of the Family Rosary Crusade may be productive of even more abundant spiritual fruits.[4]

In 1967 the friends and associates of Fr Peyton in Albany, New York hosted a twenty-fifth anniversary dinner on 21 November with seven hundred guests present. President Lyndon Johnson conveyed his congratulations by telegram.

Peyton delighted in the success of his ministry, not for himself, but for its promotion of the family and devotion of Mary. But, like everybody else, he was not immune to sorrow or the pain of loss. On 19 February 1964 Francis Wood, the Albany priest who was the first to join the Crusade effort, died. In a letter to his bishop, Fr Peyton described him as the 'perfect priest, fervent champion of Our Lady and outstanding promoter of the Family Crusade.'[5] Just a year later he experienced the loss of his brother-in-law Michael Gallagher, husband of his sister Beatrice, who died while Peyton was in the Philippines attending to matters concerning the Popular Mission. Michael and Beatrice had provided a home for him and his brother Tom upon their arrival in Scranton, a kindness he had never forgotten. Peyton wrote to console his sister: 'Now that your dear partner has gone home ahead of you, you must feel very lonely, dear Beatrice. But thanks to our father and mother, who gave to us all – their children – the equipment, the training, and the faith to accept and respond to this wish of God.'[6]

The death of Michael caused him to reflect on his family, whom he loved but barely saw, because of the demands of his work. He had expressed his thought on this matter to his sister Mary previously, telling her that what he accomplished for the Blessed Mother did not allow him time to write, but he hoped her 'delicate heart and soul understood this'.[7]

During the 1960s Peyton was also plagued by health problems. At the end of 1968 he was ordered by his doctor to take six months' rest, which he did. But he was eager to resume work, telling Grace that with medication, 'I will be able to continue as in the past, working without let up.'[8]

By the end of the decade, however, he was back in hospital again, under orders to take another two months of total rest.

CHAPTER 11

VATICAN II AND
THE CRUSADE

The Second Vatican Council, which was announced by
Pope John XXIII on 25 January 1959, began its
deliberations officially on 11 October 1962. In calling the
council – the twenty-first such assembly in the history of
the Church – the pope wished to promote ecumenism, to
bring the Church into the modern world and to
encourage a more pastoral approach to living the faith.

The sixteen documents which the council promulgated
had a profound effect on the whole Church, leading to
reform in liturgy, ecumenical dialogue, an increased role
for the laity, and a greater pastoral approach to the needs
of the People of God. As a result, Fr Peyton had to
critically examine the Family Rosary Crusade, updating
its approach and theology to conform to the council's
teaching. He had, however, no doubts about the
continuing relevance of family prayer and the Rosary, a
view he shared with the distinguished theologian, Karl
Rahner SJ who wrote: 'If the family were no longer able
to pray together, neither would the Church community
any longer be genuinely capable of doing so. If there will
always be a praying Church, then the domestic sanctuary
of the Church – the home – will likewise remain, and with
it the hope of preserving the Family Rosary.'[1]

Father Peyton went to Rome frequently between 1962 and 1965, making sure to attend the entire final session of the council, between October and December 1965. During this period, he met with the council fathers, asking their opinions on family prayer and seeking their guidance on the future of the Crusade, as well as lobbying strongly to have statements on family prayer included in the final documents. Among his allies was Cardinal Leo Jozef Suenens, who had been the auxiliary bishop of Malines-Brussels in Belgium when Peyton first showed the Rosary films at the Brussels World Fair and when the crusade came to the region in 1959. Also advising him were Mark McGrath CSC, Bishop of Santiago de Veraguas in Panama, and the Redemptorist priest and theologian, Bernard Haring CSsR.

Father Peyton enjoyed the opportunities for discussion and debate with bishops and theologians at social gatherings during the council, especially in the company of Cardinal Suenens. He wrote:

> One of the most moving and edifying of my experiences in Rome during the council was to spend an evening with Cardinal Suenens. This extraordinary man, one of the decisive influences on the entire direction and achievement of the council, drew to his lodgings the cream of the great men gathered as council fathers and advisers. The conversation, always brilliant, changed according to the people and the circumstances ... The evening would start with concelebrated Mass. Then would come a social interval to relax with the cardinal's

hospitality and meet the other guests before sitting down to a modest dinner. And at the end of dinner, the recitation of five decades of the Rosary, followed by the sung *Salve Regina*. Participating in this family gathering inspired me to a new enthusiasm, to a new conviction that not only has the Rosary survived the council, but that it has been projected to a new pinnacle of importance in the Church.[2]

With the help of Bishop McGrath and Robert Pelton CSC, Peyton drafted the following statement which was included in the Pastoral Constitution of the Church in the Modern World (*Gaudium et Spes*): 'Inspired by the example and family prayer of their parents, children, and in fact everyone living under the family roof, will more easily set upon the path of a truly more human training, of salvation, and of holiness.'[3]

Father Peyton also succeeded in having a further statement on family prayer included in the Decree on the Apostolate of the Laity as follows: 'The mission of being the primary vital cell of society has been given to the family by God himself. This mission will be accomplished if the family, by the mutual affection of its members and by family prayer, presents itself as a domestic sanctuary of the Church.'[4]

Peyton received unexpected support in this effort by Bishop Herbert Bednorz of Poland, who spoke on the council floor promoting family prayer and mentioning both Peyton and his crusade. Bednorz stated that the family could be a domestic sanctuary of the Church only through the spiritual piety of its members and through common prayer. His comments then became more specific, 'Family prayer – which in our times Fr Peyton of the Congregation of the Holy Cross stresses with such insistence in his Crusades – so intrinsically unites the family that the children most willingly turn to it: nowhere else are they more at home in a good Christian family.'[5]

The superior general, Germain Lalande CSC, reported to Richard Sullivan CSC (Peyton's provincial), that the Rosary priest's significant efforts in lobbying the bishops had paid off. 'He was for us a source of comfort and a splendid example of hard dedicated work and a profound spirit of prayer.'[6]

Father Peyton was very happy with what he described as 'the magnificent chapter' in the Council's Dogmatic Constitution of the Church (*Lumen Gentium*.) He was particularly pleased with the statement, 'This union of the Mother with the Son in the work of salvation is made manifest from the time of Christ's virginal conception up to his death.'[7] He was, however, overjoyed that Pope Paul, when promulgating the council's document on 21 November 1964, bestowed on Mary the new title of 'Mother of the Church'. The pontiff declared:

> Therefore, for the glory of the Virgin Mary and for our own consolation, we proclaim the Most Blessed Mary Mother of the Church, that is to say, of all the people of God, the faithful as well as the pastors, who call her the most loving Mother. And we wish that the Mother of God should be still more honoured and invoked by the entire Christian people by this most sweet title …[8]

Father Peyton likened Mary's role in the Church to that of the mother of any family, who pours herself out in selfless love for her children. It is noteworthy that Marshall McLuhan, the Canadian philosopher and intellectual, in an interview with Fr Peyton, described the Church as the 'all nourishing mother'.

Father Peyton arranged for his fifteen Rosary films to be shown in English, French, Spanish and Portuguese between 12 November and 4 December 1965 in the San Pietro Cinema of the Vatican. He was pleased when any bishop viewed them but was most interested in attracting bishops from missionary countries, hoping that they might purchase the films for use at home or even request a Crusade.

While Fr Peyton was very well pleased with the inclusion of his statements in two key council documents, he must have been concerned at the fall from prominence of the Rosary and other popular devotions in the council documents.

Some form of the Rosary had been part of Western Catholicism for almost seven hundred years. Pope Leo XIII (1878–1903) wrote thirteen encyclicals on the Rosary and all popes since have been ardent promoters, both in their writings and by their personal example. Perhaps no one has promoted it more than the late Pope John Paul II, most especially in his Apostolic Letter, *Rosarium Virginis Mariae*.

While the Vatican Council (1962–1965) recommended a warm and fervent devotion to Mary, no reference was made to the Rosary, nor to any Marian devotion or apparition, because there were different expressions of

Marian devotion in the Eastern and Western rites of the Catholic Church. The Rosary, so characteristic of the West, is relatively unknown among Eastern Catholics.

Many Catholics concluded that the active participation in the liturgy, which the council encouraged, appeared to have replaced all devotions. They presumed that all popular devotions had to give way to the liturgy, because it was the official, communal and superior form of prayer. While the council declared the liturgy (the Eucharist and the Sacraments, etc) was 'the summit towards which the activity of the Church is directed' and 'the fount from which all her power flows', (*Constitution on the Sacred Liturgy*, 10) it did not intend to suppress popular devotions. It did, nonetheless, direct that they be reformed so that they should not appear to be something apart from the liturgy. 'Pious exercises should be consistent with the liturgical season, should be derived from the liturgy, and should lead to the liturgy, which by its nature exceeds popular devotion.'[9]

In this crisis of uncertainty, of the liturgy vis-à-vis popular devotion, Fr Peyton wrote an impassioned letter to Pope Paul VI in May 1971, in which he asked that the Family Rosary be declared a liturgical prayer. 'My heart cries out for a papal document which could take the form of an encyclical,' he wrote. 'May I beseech your holiness to enhance, enrich and raise to a higher level of efficacy the Family Rosary by proclaiming it a liturgical prayer.'[10]

The Second Vatican Council had pointed out clearly that the life of the Church centres on the liturgy, the official worship of God by the Church as the Body of Christ. The liturgy includes, above all, the Eucharist and the other six sacraments, the Divine Office, the rites of Christian burial, the dedication of a church and religious profession. Because every liturgical celebration 'is an action of Christ the priest and of his Body which is the Church,' no other form of worship can take its place: a liturgical celebration 'is a sacred action surpassing all others; no other action of the Church can equal its efficacy ...' (*Sacrosanctum C.*, 2)

Father Peyton's letter was referred to the Congregation of Divine Worship for consideration. The outcome was the publication on 2 February 1974 of an Apostolic Letter, *Marialis Cultis,* dealing with 'the role of the Blessed Virgin in the liturgy'. Pope Paul VI did not proclaim the Rosary as a liturgical prayer, as Fr Peyton had sought, but extolled it as 'a popular devotion' which also includes such practices as pilgrimages, novenas, processions, and celebrations in honour of Mary and the saints, the Angelus, the Stations of the Cross, the veneration of relics, and the use of sacramental objects, for example, medals, scapulars, holy water. Properly used, popular devotions do not replace the liturgical life of the Church, rather they extend it into daily life.

His Holiness emphasised that liturgical celebrations and the Rosary must be neither set in opposition to one another nor considered to be identical. He reaffirmed the preeminence of the liturgical rites while acknowledging that the Rosary is a practice of piety which harmonises with the liturgy.

In his apostolic letter Pope Paul describes the three essential features of the Rosary. Firstly, the Rosary is essentially a contemplative prayer, which calls for a calm recitation: 'By its nature the Rosary calls for a quiet rhythm and a lingering pace, helping the individual to meditate on the mysteries of the Lord's life as seen through the eyes of her who was closest to the Lord'.[11] Without the contemplative element, the Rosary becomes a mechanical repetition of a formula, a body without the soul. The Servite general chapter on Marian prayer concurred with this view. 'Expressions of devotion to Mary should have the same style as the Blessed Virgin: a style marked by listening, silence and reflection. Silence is not inactivity ... but the sacred environment conducive to adoration and praise of God.'[12]

Father Romano Guardini, an advisor of Pope Benedict XVI, echoing the same sentiments, speaks of the Rosary's contemplative nature as a 'sojourn' which offers a 'quite holy world that envelopes the person who is praying ... The Rosary is not a road, but a place, it has no goal but a depth. To linger in it has great compensations.'[13]

Secondly, the Rosary is both Christ-centred and Marian: 'The Rosary is a compendium of the entire Gospel, centred on the mystery of the redemptive Incarnation.'[14] It is directed toward the events of Christ's life, as seen by Mary.

The Rosary draws from the Gospel the presentation of the mysteries and its main formulas:

> As it moves from the Angel's joyful greeting and the Virgin's pious assent, the Rosary takes its inspiration from the Gospel ... In the harmonious succession of Hail Mary's, the Rosary puts before us once more a fundamental mystery of the Gospel – the Incarnation of the Word, contemplated at the

decisive moment of the Annunciation of Mary. The Rosary is thus a Gospel prayer …

Finally, since the Rosary is centred on the same mysteries celebrated in the liturgy, it is *'excellent preparation'* for, and *'a continuing echo'* of, the liturgy; the Rosary is in harmony with the liturgy.

In his exhortation Pope Paul points out several of Mary's qualities, for our edification. Mary is the *Attentive Virgin* who receives the word of God with faith (cf. Lk 1:38). She is also the *Virgin in Prayer,* who pours out her soul in expressions glorifying God (cf. Lk 1:46-55). As *Virgin Mother,* she believed, obeyed and brought forth on earth the Father's Son. She too is the perfect model of the disciple of the Lord. Mary is, finally, the *Virgin Presenting Offerings* (cf. Ex 13:11-16), who united herself to the sacrifice of her only-begotten Son. Mary is above all the example of that worship that consists in making one's life an offering to God. Father Peyton was, no doubt, very aware of all Mary's virtues and strove to emulate each of them, not least in making his life an offering to God.[15]

His Holiness does not shrink from pointing out certain attitudes of piety which are incorrect. He reminds us that Vatican II had denounced the substitution of a reliance on merely external practices for serious commitment. Another deviation is 'sterile and ephemeral sentimentality'. The late Archbishop of Tuam, Joseph Cunnane, seemed to suggest that the Irish are guilty in this respect when he wrote: 'Some streak in us – perhaps part of our Celtic heritage – makes us sometimes inclined to over-sentimentalise her.'[16] To counteract this tendency, we need a devotion to Mary's active virtues and an awareness of her strength. She was the supreme contemplative and the tenderest of mothers, but she was also the wife, housekeeper, worker and the dutiful cousin. She was '... like all mothers and above all mothers; she is strong with the strength of sacrifice and suffering, strong with a mother's sense of duty and dedication, strong with a strength which can pass on to her children.'[17]

Marialis Cultis did call for adaptations of the Rosary to be considered. Among others, Cardinal Leo Suenens proposed the Fiat Rosary with the approval of Popes Paul VI and John Paul II. The Fiat Rosary begins with a prayer to the Holy Spirit. There are nine mysteries – three from each of the joyful, sorrowful and glorious mysteries; at each mystery there are three Hail Mary's, followed by the Glory be to the Father.

But Fr Peyton found no need to change the traditional structure of the Rosary for his own personal devotion:

> It remains full of endless inspiration for me, in the form in which I learned to lisp it at my mother's knee. No matter how busy I am, no matter how many urgent business affairs call for my attention, I never let a day go by without reciting the fifteen decades. I do not feel the need to dwell on the mysteries to which the various decades are dedicated. The words of the prayer are in themselves enough to occupy my attention, enough to lift me from the distractions around to an awareness of the presence and the love of God the Father, God the Son, and God the Holy Spirit, to a

sense of joining God himself in paying honour to the woman whom he not only chose to be the Mother of his Son, but whose permission and co-operation. He requested and invited in that supreme mystery of our salvation. Even though I repeat the same words, each time they are new, because they reveal to me another facet of the mystery, that life is not long enough to explore to its depths or to exhaust.[18]

Father Peyton also spent an hour each day in prayer before the Blessed Sacrament. He also prayed very intensely before speaking at a rally. He admits that, 'beforehand, I am always terrified at the thought of the coming ordeal.' But, as he experiences his weakness, he gains strength. 'Each time I address one [a rally] it is, for me, the first time and I go through the kind of suffering which St Paul describes ... when facing tasks beyond his strength, to the point of giving up all hope.'[19] He is referring here to a passage in St Paul's Second Letter to the Corinthians:

> My grace is enough for you: my power is at its best in weakness. So I shall be very happy to make my weaknesses my special boast so that the power of Christ may stay over me, and that is why I am quite content with my weaknesses, and with insults, hardships, persecutions, and the agony I go through for Christ's sake. For it is when I am weak that I am strong. (2 Cor 12:9-10)

He remembers with Paul that all this is necessary to remind us not to trust in ourselves but in God. 'And in that way, I find strength to force my unwilling steps to the pulpit or platform so that I can give witness to the power of God.'[20]

Many who experience difficulties with some forms of the Rosary may find encouragement in the words of St Thérèse of Lisieux. In a passage which was originally omitted from her autobiography, she lamented that the communal recitation of the Rosary troubles her greatly. 'What difficulties I have had throughout my life with saying the Rosary. I am ashamed to say that the recitation of the Rosary was at times more painful than an instrument of torture.'[21]

CHAPTER 12

RENEWAL OF
THE CRUSADE

Peyton realised that his Crusade needed thorough review and revision, in the light of Vatican II. Accordingly, he commissioned the Jesuit sociologist Renato Poblete from the Bellarmine Centre for Sociological Research in Santiago, Chile, to undertake a major study of the Crusade. He wrote to a Sister of Mercy in Albany, 'We are … undertaking a study to specifically find the place of the Family Rosary in the post-conciliar world.'[1]

The review, which took place in October and November 1965, enquired how the Crusade fitted into the renewal of the pastoral work of the Church and how the religious needs of the people were met by the Crusade. It also sought the views – positive and negative – of bishops who had some experience of a Crusade. The literature and reports from the Crusades were examined. And forty bishops who had hosted Crusades were interviewed. Questionnaires were circulated and evaluated. In addition, Fr Poblete conducted four separate meetings with a group of theologians, including John Courtney Murray SJ, Jean Danielou, Yves Congar OP and Bernard Häring CSsR.

The Poblete Report outlined the positive aspects of the Crusade and the areas that required improvement. There was no doubt that the Crusades had helped families to become communities of prayer. The bishops unanimously agreed that the crusades were well organised, effective in the use of mass media, and successful in giving the laity a sense of purpose. They also praised the efficacy of the rallies and the Popular Missions. But there were areas that needed scrutiny.

Several bishops told Fr Poblete that much of the tremendous impact of a Crusade on a diocese withered away in a relatively short time. They were impressed by how the Crusade team succeeded, for example, in involving great numbers of lay men as projectionists, instructors and in the campaign for pledges, as door-to-door visitors. They regretted, however, that when the Crusade moved on to the next diocese their involvement in the life of the Church came to an end.

They felt there ought to be a better follow-up to the crusades. Great resources of manpower and money were expended on the Crusades themselves, but very little on follow-up and maintenance. Father Peyton's response was that the post-Crusade situation was not his problem, but that of each diocese concerned. He and his team started the fire, but it was up to local leadership to keep it burning.

Father Poblete's report suggested that while Fr Peyton's talks were 'extremely good as regards sincerity, honesty and conviction', it recommended that he also speak about the whole meaning of Christian life, with its spiritual and social implications. This was especially important in underdeveloped regions of the world, where the Church's social doctrine needed to be preached more openly. The report also stressed that the Rosary should not be presented as a magic potion that guarantees success to those who use it and recommended that family prayer in general should be promoted, and not just the Rosary.

Having outlined the problems facing the Crusades the report then indicated the steps that might be taken to remedy them. It recommended that its pastoral mission, and its connection to popular devotion in the wake of Vatican II, should be reviewed. All its literature, sermons, and other materials ought to be updated to correspond to the new concept of Church generated by the council. The lay catechists should provide deeper and more theologically-sound explanations of the mysteries in their Popular Mission sessions and the Crusade should be team driven. Finally, the report warned Peyton that he must beware of politicians on the extreme right with ulterior motives, who would like to use the crusade for their own political purposes.

In March 1966, Peyton and his Family Rosary Crusade team attended a major international conference, on theological issues raised by Vatican II, in Notre Dame University. Subsequently, Fr Peyton organised a further meeting of all involved in the Crusade, including Bishop Mark McGrath CSC, Renato Poblete SJ, Robert Pelton CSC, and Arthur McCormack MHM. Father Peyton also invited a few Protestant pastors and theologians to bring a more ecumenical view to the discussions.

Speakers commented that the specific purpose of the Crusade, namely, family unity through prayer, must be maintained, but the base of the Crusade needed to expand to embrace social and liturgical references and other apostolic works. The conference participants stressed that the Crusade had to use family prayer to foster liturgical prayer and social action. A fundamental change adopted was to alter the name to Crusade for Family Prayer, as opposed to Family Rosary Crusade.

In a further effort to prepare his team to meet the post-conciliar world, in January 1967 Fr Peyton and six other Holy Cross priests began a six-month course of studies in a pastoral institute in Madrid. After they had completed their course they set about reviewing and revising the Crusade's literature in the light of the council's teachings.

The freshly updated and renewed Family Prayer Crusade was held in Milwaukee, Wisconsin from 14 April to 26 May 1968. The tasks to be performed were very much the same as usual: establishing an office, preliminary meetings, the Popular Mission, all leading up to the actual crusade, which began with the bishop's pastoral letter, including the parish, school, and institutional campaign, and ending with the rally and the pledge.

Joseph Quinn CSC explained the Crusade's renewed appearance and direction as follows:

> The overall objective of the Crusade would remain the same, namely, prayer in the family for peace and unity and love in the family. The new dimension regarding the objective would be the aspect of the family reaching out as a testimony to the community at large.[2]

There were a number of innovations in the Milwaukee Crusade, the most obvious one being the name, 'Crusade for Family Prayer', moving away from the use of the word 'Rosary'. Archbishop William Cousins of Milwaukee explained the new title to his clergy:

> We repeat this is a Campaign of Family Prayer, leaving the Rosary to the countless thousands who find in it the traditional values, the comforts and consolations of earlier days, and opening at the same time the whole broad vista of family prayer in all of its forms, not omitting family participation in the great sacrificial prayer of the Mass.[3]

The Crusade also promoted neighbourhood home Masses and innovative ways of praying the 'traditional' Rosary, including the use of Scripture. Both Fr Peyton and Cousins strongly supported an emphasis on ecumenism. Father Peyton told Quinn that what he wanted was 'a practical, efficacious, operational programme that you could sell to the Anglican Bishop, the Methodist Minister and to the Jewish rabbi'.[4]

In further gestures of ecumenism, the non-Catholic religious schools were invited to participate in the school programme, and a new prayer book with prayers from various Christian traditions was introduced.

Father Peyton fully supported the ecumenical approach: 'This is my heart, this my belief, this is my love, this is my fire, this is what I try to say to all peoples: Muhammadan, Hindu, Protestant and Catholic: "pray – pray with your family and learn from experience the meaning and value of this – the family that prays together stays together."'[5] But, being ecumenical did not lessen his devotion to Mary:

'Far from de-emphasising our dear Mary, I strike out for her with all the enthusiasm that ever I had.'[6]

The Popular Mission (viewing of fifteen Rosary films followed by catechesis) which began in Latin America, but was never tried in the United States, was introduced in Milwaukee, the target being inner-city black, Hispanic, and poor white people. The rally was much less successful in Milwaukee than in previous Crusade sites, with just thirty-five thousand attending. One reason for the poor turn-out was that it clashed with Mother's Day. The Crusade received a good deal of criticism especially from those who were not pleased with the new-look approach.

A few Holy Cross priests retired from the Crusade after the Milwaukee event, including Joseph Quinn CSC, who had served the Crusade since his ordination in 1950 and was the backbone of Fr Peyton's efforts. He was replaced by Fr John Gurley CSC, whom Richard Sullivan CSC, held in high esteem. 'Father Gurley is the one hope for its (Crusade for Family Prayer) continuation and for its possibility of attracting other young men into the work; he sees the importance of the apostolate and is willing to work for it in a selfless manner.'[7]

Two non-Holy Cross priests, who joined the Crusade team, took the lead roles as local supervisors. They were Luis Armijos Valdivieso OP, from Guayaquil, Ecuador and Reinaldo Pol Yparraguirre, from San Jose, Costa Rica. Peyton praised his new team:

> Fathers Gurley, Armijos and Pol have been the catalyst for Our Lady's overwhelming success ... These men are my hope for the future leadership of

the Crusade. They are performing a truly miraculous job ... I believe I have never been so happy, uplifted and hopeful for the future of the Crusade, as I am now'[8]

In October 1969, the Crusade finally returned to Latin America, at the invitation of Cardinal Mario Casariego of Guatemala City. An estimated 1.2 million attended on the eight nights the films were shown. Gurley captured the moment: 'The Popular Mission programme is very powerful and efficacious – and this is readily seen by anyone who has an eye and interest for the pastoral needs of the faithful.'[9] A pastoral letter from the Guatemalan bishops endorsed the Vatican II approach:

> The Crusade for Family Prayer, which we begin today, is an effort of the entire Church in Guatemala – bishops, clergy, and the faithful. The Church directs this effort toward all the families of the country without exception. We make a united call to every family Catholic or non-Catholic, inviting them to pray for a holier family and a happier world. And in this way, every true Christian should become an authentic promoter of justice and peace.[10]

The rally in Guatemala City on 7 December was attended by one hundred thousand people, including forty bishops. Archbishop Mario Casariego preached at the rally, extolling the Crusade and Fr Peyton: 'Guatemala will be as one great family praying together. Here we will always pray as Fr Peyton has taught us – Fr Peyton – the modern prophet of family prayer, the humble apostle sent to us as another Elias (Elijah) to bring down on us the blessings of Our Lady of the Rosary.'[11]

The Crusade's next stop was Costa Rica, where the Popular Mission was conducted in three cities between 4 May and 12 July 1970. The principal rally was held in the capital city of San Jose on 2 August with fifty thousand in attendance. The Crusade continued to gain momentum as it moved to El Salvador and Honduras.

The Crusade in El Salvador was conducted between 7 January and 10 March 1971, with Luis Armijos OP, John Gurley CSC, and the local auxiliary bishop Óscar Romero, as local directors. Bishop Romero, a defender of the rights of the poor, met a martyr's death on 24 March 1980 and was canonised on 14 October 2018 by Pope Francis at a ceremony in Rome. The Crusade in Honduras took place between 3 May and 11 July 1971.

The Crusades in Central America were successful in raising questions on the need for the Church to assist the poor. A new atmosphere was noted among Church officials, as regards the poor. Robert Rioux CSC reported this new mentality to the superior general: 'We [the Crusade] have been successful in convincing some of the power structures in these countries that they have an obligation to alleviate the poverty of the people.'[12]

A series of Crusades for Family Prayer took place in Mexico intermittently between 1970 and 1974. The campaign started at Merida on the Yucatan Peninsula in April 1970. A rally was held on 31 May, attended by fifty thousand people. The Crusade visited eleven separate areas from Oaxaca in the south to Tijuana in the north, with stops in the large cities of Guadalajara, Hermosillo and Obregón in 1972 and Mazatlán and La Paz in 1973. Between January and June 1974 the Crusade was conducted in Mexico City, with a grand rally on 31 May, followed by a successful pledge campaign.

Father Peyton also brought the Crusade to the Holy Land in the spring of 1971. Over four hundred people, including eight Holy Cross priests, participated in an international Rosary pilgrimage. Rallies were held in Nazareth, Bethlehem, and Jerusalem in late May 1971.

CHAPTER 13

FAMILY THEATER
IN THE 1970s

The radio programmes which brought prominence to Family Theater officially ended in 1968, with the rise of film and television making radio almost redundant.

Family Theater, nevertheless, did generate some new programmes in this decade. In January 1971 a new series of one-minute radio spots was broadcast over the Mutual network, stressing the value and need for family prayer, embodied in the popular slogan, 'The world hasn't got a prayer ... without yours.' Later the spots were carried on independent stations and broadcast overseas in local translations.

In addition to these spots, seven fifteen-minute programmes featured members of the hierarchy describing their understanding and relationship with the Virgin Mary.

The Rosary films, which had been edited earlier in the two films, *The Eternal King* and *The Redeemer,* were once again repackaged into three ninety-minute films, *The Saviour* (Joyful Mysteries), *The Redeemer* (Sorrowful Mysteries), and *The Master* (Glorious Mysteries). The advent of international television live broadcasts, made possible using satellites, created a new market for Family Theater. Pope Paul VI's Christmas Midnight Mass, sponsored by Family Theater, was broadcast live from St Peter's in Rome in 1972. The ninety-minute special, aired on one hundred and thirty-one stations in the United States, brought a new degree of national exposure to Peyton's mission. Similar broadcasts were held at Easter and Christmas in 1973, each concluding with a personal message from Fr Peyton.

The most important new project for Family Theater in the 1970s was the 'A Matter of Faith' series. The programme was 'designed to recapture and refocus the spotlight on eternal values that once held it [the world] exclusively, and in so doing to reassure many that they are indeed on the right track if they believe in God, prayer and the corollaries to these.'[1]

The series of programmes, aired weekly, proved to be very successful. The Mother's Day show, which was by far the most publicised, featured Bishop Fulton J. Sheen, long retired from the popular *Life is Worth Living* television programme.

The success of *A Matter of Faith* was greatly helped by an extensive billboard advertising campaign. Family Theater's famous slogan, 'The family that prays together stays together' had first appeared on billboards in Hollywood in 1947. Smaller posters were distributed nationwide in 1960, 1963 and 1965. Beginning in 1972 Albert Heinzer CSC, under Fr Peyton's direction, worked with the Outdoor Advertising Association on a nationwide billboard campaign, promoting family prayer. The purpose of the programme was 'to keep before the travelling public the importance of wholesome family life as part of our American heritage.'[2] Advertising space was donated by the Advertising Association and posters were supplied at a reduced price. During 1972, billboards advertising Family Theater's message were erected in two hundred and fifteen cities in forty-two states.

In 1976 another three-year billboard project was launched, featuring a short slogan followed by 'The family that prays ...' The lead-in slogans included 'God makes house calls', 'God listens' and 'God answers'. The campaign was so successful that it was renewed for a second three-year period, beginning in October 1978.

In that same year a finance committee, chaired by Peter Grace, was set up to oversee the operation of 'The All for Her Fund' – an endowment fund – which was established to pay for the daily operation of the Crusade. By 1980 donations received amounted to 2.5 million dollars. In 1992, however, the Sarita Kenedy East Foundation agreed to make an annual contribution of two hundred thousand dollars for ten years to celebrate the two thousandth birthday of Christ.

Peyton, who had long promised to take the Crusade to Argentina, began working there in July 1974. Two local priests, Luis Pedro de Fornari and Enrique Imperiale, attended a six-month training course, so they could operate and supervise the crusade. The Crusades continued in Argentina on a semi-continuous basis until December 1982, reaching nineteen dioceses and attracting over five million people to the rallies. Father Peyton spoke in Paraná in December 1974, but health problems and other commitments made additional appearances impossible. Even so, the Crusade was well received, indicating there was more to the ministry than simply the charism of

Patrick Peyton. Bishop Juan Rodolfo Laise, Bishop of San Luis, praised Peyton and his work: 'Its [Crusade's] fruits have been outstanding and self-evident; and we are sure the Lord will reward you for all the benefit that the films of the Rosary have done for souls.'[3]

In August 1974 the Bolivian bishops invited Peyton to conduct a Crusade, beginning in May 1975, as part of the national celebration of one hundred and fifty years of independence. However, problems with the training of local priests, the procurement of equipment and the dubbing of films into local Indian dialects, resulted in the Crusade starting in La Paz, the capital city, only in March 1979. It continued until 6 May, having had a grand rally on 15 April. The Crusade then moved to the Archdioceses of Santa Fe in October 1979 and Sucre in January 1980, and the Diocese of Tarija in December 1979.

The Crusade returned to Mexico in 1981 to the Diocese of San Luis Potosí between March and July and to Querétaro Diocese from July to December. Both Crusades were under the leadership of John Gurley CSC, Luis Armijos OP, and Reinaldo Pol, the same team that had directed the Mexican Crusades between 1970 and 1974. As previously, rallies were well attended in both regions.

During the Crusade's thirtieth anniversary celebration, Peyton announced a new programme, 'Campaign of the Seventies', which would concentrate his efforts in North America. The new programme, which was diocesan based, placed emphasis on family and group prayer in any format, including the discussion of Scripture, spontaneous prayer, morning and evening prayers. While the printed guidelines recommended 'emphasis on the family Rosary,' the new approach emphasised the fact that the act of praying, rather than a particular form of prayer, was most important. Families were encouraged to form small prayer groups; neighbours and friends were asked to gather at least weekly, using a prayer format they found helpful. Home Masses were promoted for Catholics to bring people together in prayer. People of all faiths were welcomed to the final rally, now referred to as a Festival of Prayer.

The new Families for Prayer Crusade was formally launched in Providence, Rhode Island, between August and December 1972, as part of the diocese's centenary celebrations. An estimated nine thousand people attended the Festival of Prayer on 24 November, which was described as giving 'witness to the power of prayer to bring peace, and unity to the family and the community'.

The Crusade next moved to Joliet, Illinois, St Louis, Missouri and South Bend, Indiana, between August 1973 and May 1974. In Joliet the Crusade formed part of the diocese's silver jubilee celebrations. The campaign in South Bend was held in April and May 1974, with the Festival of Prayer taking place on the campus of the University Notre Dame on 17 May. The final Crusade of the Campaign of the Seventies was held in Puerto Rico in 1976. It became clear, following the crusades in Joliet and St Louis, that the diocesan-wide approach no longer had an appeal in North America.

In the spring of 1978 Fr Peyton, now in his seventieth year, experienced major health problems. At the beginning of May he underwent bypass surgery in Los Angeles and convalesced afterwards at the Little Sisters of the Poor home in San Pedro, California. While there he received a letter from Poland from Carol Cardinal Wojtyla, the Archbishop of Cracow, dated 26 June 1978, in answer to a letter he had sent to the bishops of the world. The future Pope wrote:

> Here in Poland we are well acquainted with the power of the Rosary. You speak of an eclipse overshadowing Our Lady in recent years; we have not experienced it yet perhaps owing to flourishing centres of pilgrimage, of which the greatest is the shrine of Our Lady in Czestochowa. There she has been venerated by all Poland for six centuries, and recently more than ever. Every year a special Rosary celebration is held daily in our church during all October, 'the Rosary month', with exposition of the Blessed Sacrament and reciting one part of the Rosary.
>
> We should certainly be happy if it could be daily recited in all our families! Hoping that your Crusade might soon embrace all the world and bring yet more spiritual fruit, I wish you the choicest of blessings on you and your movement.[4]

On 16 October 1978 Cardinal Wojtyla became Pope John Paul II and on 17 February 1979 Peyton, accompanied by Peter Grace, met the new pontiff in a private audience. On that occasion the pope referred to Peyton as 'a man of faith' and declared publicly that the Rosary was his favourite prayer. On 8 November 1979 the Holy Father was in contact with Peyton again by letter, through the Vatican Secretary of State, with words of encouragement:

His holiness wishes to encourage you in your efforts
to promote that devotion to the Virgin Mary which
is appropriate for all who are faithful followers of
her Son. He prays through your labours on behalf
of family prayer and the daily recitation of the
Rosary Christ may be more deeply loved and
joyfully praised.[5]

In the 1980s there was a new emphasis on the family. The
United States bishops dedicated 1980 as 'the year of the
family' and the United Nations declared the year to be 'the
year of the child'. In addition, a synod of bishops met in
Rome to discuss the Christian family. Father Peyton
attended the synod and contributed significantly to its
work. Cardinal Sin of Manila bore witness to Peyton's
work: 'I personally saw him motivate the synod of bishops
gathered in Rome on behalf of the Christian family in the
modern world to adopt a resolution of the need and
power of the Family Rosary to spiritualise the family.'

Peyton's lobbying bore fruit; the synod endorsed the
Rosary as a form of family prayer: 'In fulfilling these tasks
the family will be, as it were, a "domestic church," a
community of faith living in hope and love, serving God
and the entire human family. Shared prayer and the liturgy
are sources of grace for families.'[6]

Buoyed up by the support he received from the pope
and revelling in his improved health, he faced the 1980s
with renewed zeal and courage:

With the years remaining to me, health that has just
been restored to me, the decade of the eighties – the

> fifth decade of years the Lord has allowed me to work for Our Lady – I intend with all my might to make the decade of the eighties be like the fifth glorious decade of the Rosary – the crowning years of those five decades spent in her service.[7]

With the encouragement of Al Scalpone, long associated with Family Theater, Peyton turned his attention once again to filmmaking. In the space of seven years he succeeded in producing twelve films, starting with *The Most Joyful Mystery*, based on the birth of Christ, which cost three hundred and forty thousand dollars. It was well received and was aired on seventy-three stations in the United States, thirteen in Canada, and four in the Philippines.

Peyton's new project gained a significant boost when Princess Grace of Monaco agreed to participate in three films. In 1981 she narrated *The Greatest Mystery*, depicting how Easter is celebrated by various cultures throughout the world. The following year she hosted *The Seven Last Words*, filmed at the Vatican Museum and featuring a dramatisation of the crucifixion by the London Players; and *The Nativity*, filmed at the altar of St Peter's Basilica and depicting the birth of Christ.

Father Peyton obtained the services of Mother Teresa of Calcutta and the actress Helen Hayes for *The Visitation*, the mystery chosen by Mother Teresa. The narrator was Bob Newhart. Helen Hayes also featured in *The Annunciation*, which was filmed in St Patrick's Cathedral in New York, and was released in 1983.

The last six films included *The Assumption, The Coronation, The Ascension, The Descent of the Spirit,*

The Presentation and *The Finding.* The film project was completed with a television special, *The Joyful Mysteries of the Rosary*, hosted by Loretta Young.

Peyton's new films won many awards from The Southern California Motion Picture Council, while The International Film and TV Festival of New York presented its bronze award (1981) to *The Greatest Mystery* and its silver award (1982) to *The Visitation.* The Award for Excellence for Religion in the Media was presented to *The Nativity* (1983) and *The Presentation* (1987).

CHAPTER 14

THE FINAL CRUSADES

While the original Crusade format lost its relevance in North America in 1972, when the attempt to rejuvenate the campaign failed to generate sufficient interest, it continued to appeal to Catholics in other countries.

During the 1984 Eucharistic Congress in Lima, Peru Fr Peyton reintroduced the Popular Mission, financing it with a grant of three hundred thousand dollars from the Sarita Kenedy East Foundation, which was managed by Peter Grace.

The bequest funded the purchase of projectors, generators and all the accessories needed for the Popular Mission. The mission was conducted successfully first in the Archdiocese of Cusco and subsequently in the Archdioceses of Lima and Trujillo.

Interest in the Rosary Crusades continued to be very strong in the Philippines also where a seven-year campaign was conducted semi-continuously, starting in 1978. Because of his poor health Peyton was unable to attend as often as usual, though he did speak at several rallies in May and again in October 1981. 'The magical flair and charismatic charge that Peyton gave to the Crusade was once again being exhibited.'[1]

At the invitation of the Philippines hierarchy Peyton agreed to conduct a grand Crusade to climax the seven-year campaign and to mark the Marian Year of 1985.

In an unusual move from past crusades Peyton was present in the Philippines for the entire period of the campaign, from 8 September to 8 December. He regarded the grand Crusade as the greatest opportunity of his ministerial career:

> Never in all the forty-three years of working for Our Lady have I experienced such an opportunity as this for the Family Rosary Crusade. Never was there a whole nation with all the bishops of its sixty-seven dioceses, its twenty hundred parish priests and its forty-four million Catholics committed to an all-out three-month effort for the Family Rosary.[2]

The rally held on 8 December 1985, at Luneta Park, Manila attracted two million people in one of the most powerful displays of faith experienced by Peyton in his lifetime. Ferdinand Marcos, who had ruled the Philippines as a dictator since 1965, was overthrown in February 1986 in a bloodless coup that some attributed to the recent Rosary crusade, echoing events which occurred in Brazil twenty years earlier. One freelance journalist agreed that there was more to the revolution than was physically present. 'The revolution had come at just about the right time. One cannot help but see the hand of God in the events that took place, brought about by the preceding year, 1985.'[3] On 25 February forces loyal to Corazon Aquino, armed with Rosary beads, held off a squadron of Marcos' tanks. Peyton remarked on the chain of events:

> The miraculous events of those four days in late February have left in the hearts and minds and homes of millions an awareness of their Spiritual Power – a power engendered by the Rosary. It will make history. It will be told by parents to their children through ages to come.[4]

Despite his great success in the Philippines, Peyton realised that his days of active ministry were coming to an end. He explained: 'I feel I may not, because of ill-health and advancing years, be in a position to direct the Crusade for much longer and it may not be possible to have all the features of the Crusade which my team have provided for the bishops in the past.'[5]

Accordingly, Peyton now focused his attention on the production of a Crusade handbook to enable bishops to organise diocesan crusades anywhere in the world. His handbook, which was approved by Pope John Paul II, provided guidelines on every facet of the preparations, organisation, conduct and follow-up of a successful eight-week crusade. One hundred thousand copies of the book were produced and circulated throughout the world. The first US Crusade to use the manual was Stockton, California 1988. Other sites of domestic Crusades were Palm Beach, Florida, in 1990 and Sacramento, California in 1991.

In the 1980s Peyton received many personal awards. In 1980 the combined Boards of Crusade for Family Prayer,

Family Rosary and Family Theater commissioned an update of his autobiography, first published in 1967. On his seventy-fifth birthday in 1984 the city of Scranton celebrated 'Patrick Peyton Day' with a Mass celebrated by Bishop – later Cardinal Archbishop of New York – John O'Connor in the cathedral, where Peyton had served as sacristan so many years before. He was honoured also in his native county in Ireland as 'Mayo Man of the Year' in 1988, with a presentation made in the Burlington Hotel in Dublin.

At the suggestion of David Farrell CSC and Fr Peyton, Sister Gerald Hartney CSC, an accountant, was asked in 1990, to assess the financial structure of the organisations and make recommendations for restructuring. She understood the Crusade's contemporary aim as follows:

> My own interpretation of your goal at this stage is to ensure that funds donated in Mary's name will have the legal safeguards, careful stewardship, and professional management necessary to continue and expand your special mission in any continent until the end of time.[6]

Hartney presented her reorganisation plan in June 1990. A two-tier structure was recommended, with a corporate board serving as overseer of two basic corporations, Family Rosary and Family Theater. The irrevocable All for Her trust would combine the investment portfolios for both corporations as well as the investments for Family Theater and would serve as the basic economic resource for the overall corporation.

A plan devised by William Hogan CSC, which gave control of the Crusade's operation to Holy Cross, was implemented in the summer of 1990. Father Peyton had come to realise the need for Holy Cross support in his ministry. The superior general, Claude Grou CSC, sought to reassure Peyton about the new arrangements:

> We certainly share your concern since we all want to make sure that the work you have started will continue. We all agreed that the active support of the Congregation of Holy Cross will be the best guarantee for its future and we were glad to tell you of our desire to provide that support.[7]

In 1991 and 1992, Fr Peyton celebrated the golden jubilee of his ordination and the foundation of Family Rosary. The anniversary of his ordination was celebrated at Notre Dame, North Easton, Albany, Chicago, Philadelphia, in his native parish of Attymass and throughout Ireland. On Sunday 28 July 1991, Mayo County Council joined with Attymass parishioners in celebrating, with immense pride, the golden jubilee of the world-renowned Rosary Priest. Prior to a Mass of thanksgiving, Fr Peyton was presented with a formal address by the chairperson of Mayo County Council, Padraic Cosgrove, which read as follows:

> In honouring Father Patrick Peyton CSC ... Mayo County Council wish to place on formal record our admiration of his achievements ...
> ... Mindful then of your marvellous work in proclaiming Mary across the world ... we do hereby

declare Fr Patrick Peyton worthy of this special honour being conferred on him by his native county. We salute him as a noble friend and a great son of Mayo and a man worthy of the highest respect in his native land.[8] Given under the seal of Mayo County Council this twenty-eighth day of July 1991.

In his reply, Fr Peyton said, 'I am deeply moved by this honour which has been conferred on me by Mayo County Council.' He then recalled how his late father, John Peyton, repaired roads under contract for the Council, and that the money he received in payment helped to put bread on the table for a large family. Father Peyton continued, 'I have never forgotten this for Mayo County Council, and this honour conferred on me here today is so much appreciated by me.'[9]

Following the concelebrated Mass, Fr Peyton visited Ballina library where Bishop Thomas Finnegan, Bishop of Killala, formally declared open an exhibition on the life and times of Fr Peyton. In his address Bishop Finnegan stated that Fr Peyton was one of the first in the Church to realise that the mass media were ready-made and powerful instruments of evanglisation. He continued, 'As a young priest he saw radio, cinema and television carrying his dual message to millions: "The family that prays together, stays together"; and "the perfect family prayer is the Rosary." That message is as valid today as it was when Fr Peyton first began to preach it.' The bishop continued, 'During his fifty years as a priest, Fr Pat has been a man of faith, prayer and love; love of God, love of

His Blessed Mother and love of everyone he meets. That's his secret which, in the words of President Bush has enabled Fr Peyton "to draw people closer to God and to one another."'[10]

The Golden Jubilee of Family Rosary was noted by Pope John Paul II and by Mary Robinson, president of Ireland. On 11 February 1992 the Pope wrote: 'I give thanks to God for the many gifts bestowed on the Church through your tireless and persevering efforts through this half century ... I pray that all Christian families may discover the treasure of the Family Rosary in order that their family life be strengthened and blessed.'[11]

Father Peyton's heart problems became more acute, necessitating the fitting of a pacemaker in 1987 and angioplasties in 1990 and 1992. He was hospitalised on three occasions for congestive heart failure in December 1991 and in February and April 1992.

Father Peyton did not fear death. In an interview with broadcaster Gemma McCrohan for the RTÉ television documentary *A Dedicated Man* in 1990, he said that for him death was 'going home'. His words recall St Paul, who, in the letter to the Philippians declared, 'I want to be gone and to be with Christ, and this is by far the stronger desire ...' (Ph 1:23).

Back with the Little Sisters of the Poor in San Pedro, California his health continued to decline. Throughout his final illness he remained faithful to the recitation of the fifteen decades of the Rosary and, when possible, his daily Mass. On the evening of 2 June 1992, he could not finish his Rosary but was told by staff members that they would finish the prayer for him. Patrick Peyton died peacefully at 5.20 a.m. on 3 June, his last words being 'Mary, my queen, my mother'. He was laid to rest on 8 June in the Holy Cross community cemetery at Stonehill College, Massachusetts, following his funeral Mass.

The tributes to Fr Peyton were numerous and heartfelt. Archbishop John Foley, President of the Pontifical Commission for Social Communication, wrote, 'The death of Fr Patrick Peyton is a loss which will be deeply felt. He touched the lives of millions of people through radio and television with the simplicity and sincerity of his life and of his message.'[12] The superior general of Holy Cross, Claude Grou CSC, commented:

> As he departs for his final reward, Fr Peyton leaves to us all a mission to pursue. We, who have seen the importance of his work, need today to join hands and renew our commitment to pursue the task for which he has given up his life. And as we pursue this work, we know that we can count on his support and protection.[13]

In 1996, Fr Peyton was posthumously awarded the Gabriel Award for Personal Achievement by the National Association of Catholic Broadcasters in USA. The citation acknowledged him as a 'pioneer in producing radio and TV programmes to uplift the human spirit'.

The process for the canonisation of Fr Peyton began in 1997, five years after his death. The Church canonises holy people not for their own sakes, but to present them to the faithful as models of Christian life and as powerful intercessors. In their triumph over the challenges of life through faith, we are inspired to trust God more fully and to serve others more generously. The campaign achieved an initial milestone in 2001 when the Rosary Priest was named 'Servant of God,' the first formal title on the road to sainthood. In 2003, the Diocese of Fall River in Massachusetts opened an official canonisation enquiry that, due to its scope, was transferred to the Archdiocese of Baltimore in 2008.

As part of the investigation, Holy Cross priests visited the Diocese of Scranton to interview family members and collect documents, such as personal letters, that might offer insight into Fr Peyton's life. The inquiry produced six thousand pages of documentation that were eventually condensed into a thirteen-hundred-page summary of his life and ministry, known as a 'Positio'. It became the primary source that the Vatican's Congregation for the Causes of Saints considered in determining that he had lived a holy life. On 18 December 2017, Pope Francis approved the Decree of the Heroic Virtue of Fr Patrick Peyton CSC, thus bestowing on him the title of Venerable. The declaration of 'Venerable' is the last step before beatification, which requires a miracle attributed to the person's intercession.

The Posito on the life of Fr Peyton had previously been discussed and approved by a panel of theologians and subsequently by a group of fifteen cardinals and archbishops who voted to recognise his heroic virtues. Hundreds of testimonies to Fr Peyton's heroic virtue and holiness of life have been recorded.

EPILOGUE

Father Peyton was one of the great spiritual leaders of the twentieth century, an inspiring priest who spent his entire adult life in the service of family prayer; as the central object of his spiritual devotion was Mary, the central message of his spirituality was the need for family prayer through the Rosary. Although Fr Peyton himself believed that the Family Rosary was the most forceful prayer, he did promote, especially in later life, a more ecumenical and broader message that family prayer of any kind was highly desirable. His veneration of Mary, however, did not rule out other influences. Francis Grogan CSC, who worked closely with him, observed: 'I always said that he was well balanced in his spirituality. He had great devotion to Our Lady and to the Rosary, but he also had great esteem and love for the Mass, and he made a holy hour every day.'[1]

Peyton saw prayer as the essential aspect of spiritual life – an aspect that one must experience internally and then externalise in the form of virtuous actions. Ministry for him was only a manifestation of what must be happening inside. Elsewhere he describes prayer as 'an intimate experience between the person who prays and God, a living communication between two free beings based in love'.[2]

For him the essence of Christian life was the spirit of sacrifice. Peyton believed that in loving Christ we are called through Baptism to be the presence of Christ to others. Living the Christian life wasn't easy; it called for personal sacrifice. Peyton explained:

> And so my dear people, the life of Christ in you is a grand life. And if it is healthy there is a great spirit of sacrifice in you, a great spirit of self-denial, and self-surrender ... There is no other way to bridge the gap between heaven and earth except by the narrow way of the cross.[3]

The practice of the Catholic faith in Ireland has declined steeply in recent years. While 78 per cent of people still identify as Catholic, in recent surveys it appears that only 30 per cent attend Sunday Mass on a regular basis. The late Michael Paul Gallagher SJ once suggested that God was 'missing but not missed' in contemporary Ireland, which had moved from alienation towards the institutional Church, through anger at the abuse scandals of the 1990s, to apparent apathy. But that apathy could be 'a mask on suppressed hunger'.[4] The human person hungers for meaning, for inner peace and for hope. In *Evangelii Gaudium* (The Joy of the Gospel), Pope Francis teaches that it is the mission of the Church, and all its members – since we are all called to be evangelisers – to proclaim the life-giving message of the Gospel, which alone brings authentic fulfilment; our friendship in faith with Jesus 'sets us free from sin, sorrow, inner emptiness and loneliness'.[5]

Pope Francis declares that we have been entrusted with the Good News, a treasure which makes us more human and helps us to lead a new life. 'There is nothing more precious which we can give to others. The Gospel message ... responds to our deepest needs since we were created for what it offers us. This message will speak to the deepest yearnings of people's hearts.'[6] It should rightly disturb and trouble our consciences as '... so many of our brothers and sisters are living without the strength, light and consolation born of friendship with Jesus Christ; without a community of faith to support them; without meaning and a goal in life.'[7]

All the energies of the Church should be channelled for the evangelisation of today's world rather than for her self-preservation. Christians must regard the lapsed and unbelieving with the utmost compassion while, at the same time, reaching out to them at every opportunity. Every parish and diocese must cultivate a sense of mission, a sense of responsibility for the spread of the Gospel. Father Peyton's sense of mission led him to make a total commitment to his work, pursuing his goal with a holy passion. His remarkable courage and zeal should help inspire and motivate modern day workers in the vineyard, to go forth to preach the Gospel without hesitation, reluctance or fear.

ENDNOTES

Introduction
1. Michael Maher, *Irish Spirituality,* Dublin: Veritas Publications, 1981, p. 7.
2. Patrick Peyton, *All for Her,* California: Family Theater Inc 1967, p. 147.
3. Theodore Bonnet, *Father Peyton and God, Family Digest* 8 January 1953.
4. Michael Maher, *Irish Spirituality.* op. cit. p. 5.
5. Ibid. p. 5.

Chapter 1: The Early Years
1. Stephen Purkis, *Famine in Attymass*, Attymass Parish, 2017, p. 10.
2. Liam Swords, *In their Own Words,* Dublin: Columba Press, 1999, p. 92.
3. Ibid. p. 236.
4. Stephen Purkis, *Famine in Attymass.* op. cit. p. 11.
5. *The Nation Newspaper*, Dublin, 5 June 1847.
6. Patrick Peyton, *All for Her,* op. cit. p. 8.
7. T. W. Moody, F. X. Martin, *The Course of Irish History,* Cork: Mercier Press, 1984, p. 289.
8. Patrick Peyton, *All for Her,* op. cit. p. 16.
9. Ibid. p. 16.
10. Ibid. p. 7.

11. Richard Gribble, *American Apostle of the Family Rosary,* New York: The Crossroad Publishing Company, 2005, p. 17.
12. Ibid. p. 338 n. 38.
13. Ibid. p. 16.
14. Patrick Peyton, *All for Her,* op. cit. p. 25.
15. Liam Swords, *A Hidden Church*, Dublin: Columba Press, 1997, p. 280.
16. www.Irisharstreview.com/decoration-and-decorum
17. Peter O'Dwyer, *Mary: A History of Devotion in Ireland,* Dublin: Four Courts Press, 1998.
18. Peter O'Dwyer, *Towards a History of Irish Spirituality,* Dublin: Columba Press, pp. 41, 42.
19. Ibid. p. 42.
20. Padraic Ó Fiannachta, *Saltair,* Dublin: Columba Press, 1988, p. 87.
21. Michael Maher, *Irish Spirituality.* op. cit. p. 54.
22. Patrick Peyton, *All for Her,* op. cit. p. 11.
23. W. B. Yeats, 'An Irish Airman Foresees his Death', *The Wild Swans at Coole,* London: Macmillan, 1973.

Chapter 2: Exiles in America

1. Patrick Peyton, *All for Her.* op. cit. pp. 27, 28.
2. Ibid. p. 36.
3. Jeanne Gosselin Arnold, *A Man of Faith*, California: Family Theatre, Inc, 1983, p. 12.
4. Patrick Peyton, *All for Her.* p. 44.
5. Richard Gribble, *American Apostle of the Family Rosary,* p. 20.
6. Patrick Peyton, *All for Her.* op. cit. p. 45.
7. Richard Gribble, *American Apostle of the Family Rosary,* p. 20, 21.
8. Ibid. p. 23.

9. Ibid. p. 23.
10. Patrick Peyton, *All for Her*, p. 45.
11. Richard Gribble, *American Apostle of the Family Rosary*, p. 22.
12. Ibid. p. 114.
13. Ibid. p. 114.
14. Ibid. p. 24.
15. Patrick Peyton, *All for Her*, p .61.
16. Patrick Peyton, *All for Her*, p. 72.
17. Ibid. p. 72.
18. Ibid. p. 74.
19. Ibid. p. 76.
20. Ibid. p. 75.
21. Ibid. p. 75.
22. Ibid. p. 75.
23. Ibid. p. 77.

Chapter 3: Promoting the Family Rosary

1. Richard Gribble, *American Apostle of the Family Rosary*, op. cit. p. 40.
2. Ibid. p. 39.
3. Ibid. p. 39.
4. Patrick Peyton, *All for Her*, op. cit. p. 85.
5. Richard Gribble, *American Apostle of the Family Rosary*, op. cit. p. 43.
6. Ibid. p. 45.
7. Ibid. p. 44.
8. Ibid. p. 44.

Chapter 4: Family Theater of the Air

1. Patrick Peyton, *All for Her,* op. cit. p. 103.
2. Richard Gribble, *American Apostle of the Family Rosary,* op. cit. p. 50.
3. Ibid. p. 53.
4. Ibid. pp. 53, 54.
5. Patrick Peyton, *All for Her,* op. cit. p. 114.
6. Richard Gribble, *American Apostle of the Family Rosary,* op. cit. p. 55.
7. Ibid. p. 55.
8. Ibid. pp. 55, 56.
9. Ibid. p. 58.
10. Ibid. p. 58.
11. Ibid. p. 58.
12. Ibid. p. 59.
13. Ibid. p. 61.
14. Patrick Peyton, *All for Her,* op. cit. p. 267.
15. Ibid. p. 268.
16. Richard Gribble, *American Apostle of the Family Rosary,* op. cit. p. 69.
17. Ibid. p. 70.
18. Ibid. p. 71.
19. Ibid. pp. 71, 72.
20. Ibid. p. 7.

Chapter 5: Birth of the Rosary Crusade

1. Patrick Peyton, *All for Her,* op. cit. p. 143.
2. Richard Gribble, *American Apostle of the Family Rosary,* op. cit. p. 112.
3. Ibid. p. 105.
4. Patrick Peyton, *All for Her,* op. cit. p. 147.
5. Ibid. p. 147.

6. Richard Gribble, *American Apostle of the Family Rosary,* op. cit. p. 111.
7. Patrick Peyton, *All for Her,* op. cit p. 147.
8. Richard Gribble, *American Apostle of the Family Rosary,* op. cit. p. 108.
9. Ibid. p. 108.
10. Ibid. p. 367 n. 37.
11. Ibid. p. 126.
12. Ibid. p. 116.
13. Ibid. pp. 117, 118.
14. Ibid. pp. 118, 119.
15. Ibid. p. 120.
16. Patrick Peyton, *Ear of God,* Garden City, N.Y.: Doubleday, 1951, p. VIII.
17. Richard Gribble, *American Apostle of the Family Rosary,* op. cit. p. 120.
18. Ibid. p. 12.
19. Jeanne Gosselin Arnold, *A Man of Faith,* pp. 99, 100.

Chapter 6: The Irish Crusade

1. Patrick Peyton, *All for Her,* op. cit. p. 175.
2. Ibid. p. 173.
3. Ibid. p. 173.
4. Ibid. p. 175.
5. *Irish Independent,* Souvenir of Fr Peyton's Rosary Crusade in Ireland, 1954.
6. Ibid.
7. Patrick Peyton, *All for Her,* op. cit. p. 175.
8. Ibid. p. 175.
9. *Irish Independent,* Souvenir of Fr Peyton's Rosary Crusade in Ireland, 1954.
10. Patrick Peyton, *All for Her,* op. cit. p. 175.

11. Richard Gribble, *American Apostle of the Family Rosary,* op. cit. p. 125.
12. Ibid. pp. 124, 125.
13. Ibid. p. 331.

Chapter 7: Asian and African Campaigns

1. Richard Gribble, *American Apostle of the Family Rosary,* op. cit. p. 126.
2. Ibid. p. 126.
3. Ibid. p. 373.
4. Jeanne Gosselin Arnold, *A Man of Faith*, 1983, pp. 120–121.
5. Richard Gribble, *American Apostle of the Family Rosary,* op. cit. p. 127.

Chapter 8: Crusade under Scrutiny

1. Father Peyton, *All for Her,* op. cit. p. 203.
2. Ibid. p. 201.
3. Ibid. p. 203.
4. Ibid. p. 203.
5. Ibid. p. 203.
6. Richard Gribble, *American Apostle of the Family Rosary,* p. 128.
7. Ibid. p. 128.

Chapter 9: Latin-American Crusades 1959–66

1. Father Peyton, *All for Her*, op. cit. p. 220.
2. Ibid. p. 220.
3. Ibid. p. 220.
4. Ibid. p. 222.

5. Richard Gribble, *American Apostle of the Family Rosary,* op. cit. p. 178.
6. Ibid. p. 164.
7. Ibid. p. 178.
8. Ibid. p. 180.
9. Ibid. p. 182.
10. Ibid. p. 183.
11. Jeanne Gosselin Arnold, *A Man of Faith*, op. cit. pp. 187, 188.
12. Richard Gribble, *American Apostle of the Family Rosary,* p. 185.
13. Ibid. p. 186.
14. Ibid. p. 187.
15. Ibid. p. 187.
16. Ibid. p. 188.
17. Ibid. p. 188.
18. Ibid. p. 190.
19. Ibid. p. 190.
20. Ibid. p. 191.
21. Ibid. p. 191.
22. Ibid. p. 191.
23. Ibid. p. 191.
24. Ibid. p. 191.
25. Ibid. p. 191.

Chapter 10: Bringing Christ to the Masses

1. Richard Gribble, *American Apostle of the Family Rosary,* op. cit. p. 208.
2. Ibid. p. 208.
3. Ibid. p. 210.
4. Ibid. p. 211.
5. Ibid. p. 212.
6. Ibid. p. 212.

7. Ibid. p. 212.
8. Ibid. pp. 212, 213.

Chapter 11: Vatican II and the Crusade
1. Richard Gribble, *American Apostle of the Family Rosary,* op. cit. p. 247.
2. Patrick Peyton, *All for Her,* op. cit. pp. 253, 254.
3. Richard Gribble, *American Apostle of the Family Rosary,* op. cit. p. 249.
4. Ibid. p. 249.
5. Ibid. p. 249.
6. Ibid. p. 249.
7. Patrick Peyton, *All for Her,* op. cit. p. 239.
8. Paul VI, 21/11/64, Closing of Vatican II.
9. Paul VI, *Marialis Cultus.*
10. '*Rosary since Vatican II*', University of Dayton, Ohio.
11. Servites' General Chapter on Marian Prayer.
12. Ibid.
13. Romano Guardini, *Rosary since Vatican II,* University of Dayton, Ohio.
14. Paul VI, *Marialis Cultus,* paragraph 44.
15. Ibid. p. 68.
16. Joseph Cunnane, *Mother of the Redeemer,* ed. K. McNamara, Dublin, 1959, p. 303.
17. Ibid. p. 303.
18. Patrick Peyton, *All for Her,* op. cit. p. 254.
19. Ibid.
20. Ibid. p. 148.
21. 'Rosary since Vatican II', University of Dayton, Ohio.

Chapter 12: Renewal of the Crusade

1. Richard Gribble, *American Apostle of the Family Rosary,* op. cit. p. 251.
2. Ibid. p. 255.
3. Ibid. p. 256.
4. Ibid. p. 256.
5. Ibid. p. 256.
6. Ibid. p. 257.
7. Ibid. pp. 258, 259.
8. Ibid. p. 259.
9. Ibid. p. 260.
10. Ibid. p. 260.
11. Ibid. p. 260.
12. Ibid. p. 261.

Chapter 13: Family Theater in the 1970s

1. Richard Gribble, *American Apostle of the Family Rosary,* op. cit. p. 268.
2. Ibid. p. 269.
3. Ibid. p. 273.
4. Jeanne Gosselin Arnold, *A Man of Faith,* op. cit. p. 250, 251.
5. Ibid. p. 254.
6. Richard Gribble, *American Apostle of the Family Rosary,* op. cit. p. 306.
7. Ibid. p. 307.

Chapter 14: The Final Crusades

1. Richard Gribble, *American Apostle of the Family Rosary,* op. cit. p. 310.
2. Ibid. p. 311.
3. Ibid. p. 311.

4. Ibid. p. 311.
5. Ibid. p. 312.
6. Ibid. p. 316.
7. Ibid. p. 317.
8. Padraic Cosgrave, chairperson, Mayo County Council, Golden Jubilee Celebration.
9. Richard Gribble, *American Apostle of the Family Rosary,* op. cit. p. 318.
10. Bishop Thomas Finnegan, *The Western People,* 7 August 1991.
11. Richard Gribble, *American Apostle of the Family Rosary,* op. cit. p. 318.
12. Ibid. p. 319.
13. Ibid. p. 319.

Epilogue
1. Richard Gribble, *American Apostle of the Family Rosary,* op. cit. p. 324.
2. Ibid. p. 325.
3. Ibid. p. 325.
4. *The Irish Times*, Dublin, 8 August 2004.
5. Pope Francis, *Evangelii Gaudium,* 1.
6. Ibid. pars. 264, 265.
7. Ibid. par. 49.

BIBLIOGRAPHY

Arnold, Jeanne Gosselin, *A Man of Faith*, Albany, New York: Family Theater Inc, 1983.

Corish, Patrick, *The Irish Catholic Experience*, Dublin: Gill and Macmillan, 1986.

Gribble, Richard CSC, *American Apostle of the Family Rosary*, New York: Crossroad Publishing Co., 2005.

Flannery, Austin OP, *Vatican Council II*, Dublin: Dominican Publications, 1975.

Foley, Jack, *Swinford Spalpeens*, Ardfield, Co. Cork, 2017.

Maher, Michael MSC, *Irish Spirituality*. Dublin: Veritas Publications, 1981.

Moody T.W. & Martin, F.X., *The Course of Irish History*, Cork: The Mercier Press, 1984.

O'Dwyer, Peter, *Towards a History of Irish Spirituality*, Dublin: Columba Press, 1995.

O'Dwyer, Peter, Mary: *A History of Devotion in Ireland*, Dublin: Four Courts Press, 1998.

Ó Fiannachta, Pádraig, *Saltair*, Dublin,: The Columba Press, 1988.

Ó Ríordáin, John J., CSsR, *Irish Catholic Spirituality*, Dublin: The Columba Press, 1998.

Pope Francis, *Evangelii Gaudium*, London: Catholic Truth Society 2013.

Pope Paul VI, *Marialis Cultus*, Athlone: St Paul Publications 1994.

Peyton, Patrick CSC, *All for Her,* California: Family Theater Publications, 1967.

Peyton, Patrick, CSC, *The Ear of God,* Garden City, N.Y.: Doubleday, 1954.

Reynolds, Sean, *Golden Jubilee 1941 – 1991.* Attymass, Ballina, 1991.

Swords, Liam, *A Hidden Church,* Dublin: The Columba Press, 1997.

Swords, Liam, *A Dominant Church*, Dublin: The Columba Press, 2004.